Getting God Wrong

Getting God Wrong

G. S. KOHLER

WIPF & STOCK · Eugene, Oregon

GETTING GOD WRONG

Wipf & Stock
An Imprint of Wipf and Stock Publishers
199 W. 8th Ave., Suite 3
Eugene, OR 97401

www.wipfandstock.com

PAPERBACK ISBN: 978-1-6667-6478-9
HARDCOVER ISBN: 978-1-6667-6492-5
EBOOK ISBN: 978-1-6667-6493-2

10/04/23

For Beckie
Who taught me to listen
carefully, and to pray always.

Contents

Acknowledgments

*I want to acknowledge the help
of Annie Carmitchell who wondered aloud, read, and suggested,
Dr. Roger Green who read and advised,
Sandy, who wanted God to be relevant,
Maggie, who persevered through love,
and Walter, who asked the
best questions.*

Introduction

Saying something over and over can make it seem true, but it just seems true. It does not make it true. Politicians and older brothers and sisters have tried that trick forever. And for centuries we have told each other the meaning and nature of the words of the Bible, with a sense that we were very clear on how God spoke to us. This brief book, which may be revolutionary to some but simply supportive to others, does not challenge the words but the way we have taught ourselves to hear the tone of voice of the Bible, essentially God's voice. In doing that it can also challenge portraits, sermons, impressions and even fast-held beliefs about God, as people told each other how to hear the God that is presented in the Old Testament and the New Testament. It questions translations gently and suggests that some of this work has been based more on tradition than on engagement with the circumstance and context of the words. It may also provide a different thought and experience for those who have walked away from God because of how they were taught to hear God.

Fundamentally, this is a book that challenges judgment, and it suggests we would do well to give up judging. Jesus told us not to judge because we had no ability to do it at all, let alone well. The only one who can do it is God, because God is the one who knows the truth. So this is a book that reconsiders how God sees, hears, and speaks and how our response should be to learn rather than to judge.

I asked my mom one day why we chose our church. "How did we end up there?" She said, "Oh, your dad picked it. He said, 'That's where they preach the Gospel,' so we went there." I asked her the question because I had become convinced, after my own conversion, that my father not only was not a *real* Christian, but he probably needed to hear the gospel for the first time. I had spent nearly two years pounding on that guy, with every clever point I could imagine, to get him to turn his life over to Jesus. My mom's explanation kicked me back on my heels. I realized that I wasn't really looking for my dad to find Jesus. I was looking for him to find Jesus the same way I did.

I started looking at my dad and myself in a whole new way that day. My dad's silent patience with me, his putting up with and listening to all the stuff I put him through without arguing, humbled me. It made me look at myself and my relationship with him, the rest of the world, and God in a whole new way. I began to see and hear my dad's commitment to Jesus in my reawakened memories and in conversations. My arrogance became vivid and crushing, and it made me begin to turn toward God's grace, seeking to know and understand God more sincerely.

Not long after that personal revelation, away at my conservative Christian college, I was studying a book that was being challenged by members of the student body. It was a book written by a well-known Jewish rabbi. The questioning demand of these students was "Why are we studying a Jewish writer?" That brought it to a faculty review board. The book's use was defended and kept in the curriculum, and some students opted out of the class, but I stuck and was reading it.

The book was about God's grace and this one evening, as I read in the Research (the *quiet*) Room of our library, I stopped taking notes and just read. I had gotten lost in the overwhelmingly wondrous and insightful perception, and I began to cry. I felt God close by at that moment and I started to talk with God through my tears. I asked, "How are you going to send this guy to hell? He understands your grace way better than I do. He gets you." I was taught and was convinced that everyone who did not accept Jesus as Savior and Lord, was going to hell. Not only that, but I just accepted that the way I'd come to faith was the way everyone should come. That is what drove me to condemn my own father, and it was basis of the arrogance I carried in relating to the world.

I sat for a while holding this book that challenged—*rocked*—all my understanding of judgment, and my responsibility to hold others in condemnation. At the end of about 20–30 minutes, I gave up. I gave up my need to judge. Essentially, as I was sitting there in God's presence, hearing the Holy Spirit ask "what do you think you're supposed to be doing here?" I knew I was charged with doing something other than to decide who around me was going to hell. I sat thinking through the requirement I felt, to base my own clarity of God's love for me on the assurance that there were some who not only got God wrong, but in getting God wrong, were my and God's enemies, against whom I should fight, and were doomed to hell. That last thought had given me assurance that I didn't need to spend any time thinking of them as important or as persons. They were lost . . . well, unless they came to God the way I instructed them to come to God.

This all made me wonder if I was the one getting God wrong. Over time and the more I considered all this, it became clear to me that I was not here to condemn or to figure out who was in and who was out. My job was to follow Jesus, to love God with all my heart, mind, soul, and strength and to love other people. It has been said before, but, when we figure out that the main point of our lives is to love God and to love others then everything else sort of falls into place.

As our news feeds bring to light more and more abuse, armed attacks, mistreatment, failure, scandals, cover-ups, and neglect, as we see seemingly faithful people tie their integrity to political power, more and more Christians are foundering in their faith, and more people are just sliding into a "spiritual but not religious" perspective. Throughout our society people are missing God, either by choice, confusion, or indifference. If God ever had a place in their lives, it is not one to which they can find their way back. And Christians do not seem to be helping them. People in our society no longer recognize Jesus' followers by their love for each other but by their hypocrisy, or their anger, or hatred, or thoughtless rejection of others. This speaks to how Christians are forgetting what they discovered in being found by Jesus, the core need we have as human beings for God's love and peace.

Throughout history, people have recognized or discovered a need for God. Famous quotes echo this need:

> "You have made us for yourself, O Lord, and our heart is restless until it rests in you." —Augustine of Hippo[1]

> "There is a God-shaped vacuum in the heart of each man which cannot be satisfied by any created thing but only by God the Creator, made known through Jesus Christ." —Blaise Pascal[2]

> "If we find ourselves with a desire that nothing in this world can satisfy, the most probable explanation is that we were made for another world." —C. S. Lewis[3]

---

1. Augustine, Book 1, para. 1.
2. Pascal, *Pensées*, 142.
3. Lewis, *Mere Christianity*, 136–37.

Right now, many in our world are saying that the spiritual experience they are having seems empty. Bruce Springsteen, Douglas Coupland and Kurt Cobain are recent, yet historic, poet-examples of those who all talk about seeking for an answer and finding an empty sky. They speak for generations as well as communities of people. They seem to ask, "What if I've tried church, tried meditation, tried drugs, tried sex, tried the various religions, and tried just being good, at least good enough for my standards, what then? What if I look up and regardless of whether it is cloudy or clear . . . it just seems empty . . . ?"

Sitting in the quiet room of the Library that night, I was challenged in my view of what I was told the Bible is saying. It made me go back to look at the principal words we use, Scriptures we offhandedly reference as if we know everything they say and mean. I needed to dig through all the religious complications I had learned to find Jesus. Now you may be saying, "I tried Jesus, when I was trying all the other stuff." I thought I had too, but this walk has led me to find, even more deeply, the one who loves me best.

The thing I found most in all this is where I've gotten God wrong. It is made me consider that maybe the Bible is the history of people getting God wrong. If you think that is messed up, well, welcome to the conversation.

Chapter One

I Used to Think the Most Important Thing to God Was Obedience

MY CHILDREN GREW UP hiking and camping with me. I've always loved it. Once, my son, Sam, and I took a trip to Denali National Park in Alaska to hike in the wilderness. Sam was an adult at this time. We found ourselves, one day, coming down a mountain using a goat trail. Goat trails are made by small hooves and not human feet, so the path was pretty narrow. The side of the mountain above and below us was loose rock, just loose rock. They call it "scree," and if you slip and fall there's a good chance you do not stop until you hit the valley floor hundreds of feet below. There's nothing to grip or catch because the rocks will just keep sliding away from you.

Sam was ahead of me, and I saw his natural inclination was to lean into the mountain beside him. We were carrying these enormous backpacks, and Sam kept leaning over, reaching in toward the mountainside. Naturally, he felt like laying his hand on the mountain would make him safer, but he was doing the most dangerous thing he could do.

As he leaned off to his side to put his hand on the mountain, he was shifting his balance and the angle of his body. He was lining himself up with the angle of the mountainside and, with the slightest misstep or slip, he would be tumbling down the mountain. As I walked behind him, I kept calling to him to "stand up straight," and "Sam, listen to me. You have to straighten up!" He finally listened, but that meant he had to refuse to follow his clearest instinct, to put his hand on something close for security, to lean into what felt safe. He had to walk upright, just the way goats do, the way the path went.

My words at that moment could sound like an order. I am his father, calling out a command, demanding obedience. But I did not experience it that way. That wasn't my tone of voice. I experienced it as seeing something Sam couldn't and giving him instruction.

The Bible tells us in Prov 3:5–6,

> Trust in the Lord with all your heart
> and *lean not* on your own understanding;
> in all your ways submit to him,
> and he will make your paths straight.

We have told ourselves that God gave us commands by which to live, but what if God was giving us instructions? What if God's words to us were not a list of commandments but guidelines, instructions on how to live well? In cultures around the world, we have created a sense of a demanding God who is offended at our missteps and lashes out against those who disobey his laws. In some ways, we have taught ourselves that God is a mean and shallow individual who suddenly changes when we come to the New Testament. So many people in the world have reacted against this image because it challenges reasoning. Why would the God of the Old Testament be this demanding ogre while Jesus was kind and loving?

Take the *His Dark Materials* series of books for children, where a fantasy world is created by Philip Pullman in order to create a place where God can be revealed as this shriveled, angry, creaturely figure who can be destroyed, killed off as unneeded anymore. The imagery Pullman uses, of a child, the heroine's best friend, being sacrificed summarily on a treasure/power hunter's whim to reach his goal suggests that this attack on a "historical" and Christian image of God is direct. Isn't this what Christianity is teaching? Hasn't it been teaching that God is a controlling person who plays with people's lives, and, ultimately, must kill his son to get his way. The "god" of *His Dark Materials* is revealed as worthless and weak and one who should be rejected. The point I am making here is that people have been taught that God is a demanding tyrant, and when Jesus enters, it appears like he has never read what we read in the Old Testament. And then, we've been told, he is killed off to placate an angry God.

In the December 1, 2007, issue of *The Atlantic*, we're told that "when pressed Pullman grants that he's not really trying to kill God, but rather the outdated idea of God as an old guy with a beard in the sky."[1] That may be

---

1. Rosin, "How Hollywood Saved God," para. 17.

true, but it may also be that this was an image of which God never had a part. And if that is so, then pushing people away from that image but not toward anything more than the "dust" that surrounds Pullman's characters at adolescence is providing them and us with little hope in the world. Instead of providing a clearer image of God, we are left with a sense that there is a "magic" in the world that helps people sometimes.

I get why people are frustrated by the image of God that's been presented to us. Not just atheists but faithful people, over many years, have taught themselves to seek safety in control and in a God who demands control, rather than the God who is fully in love with the world and doesn't control things like a big human being. We love control. Safety has become our primary concern, and it is found in our creating borders, parameters, and rules of purity or holiness that may never have been God's desire for us. It's found in our assurance of being able to judge and even to condemn others. Instead of listening to God, we may have made safety or even purity our god.

WHAT MAKES US FEEL SAFE AND WHY MIGHT THAT NOT BE GOOD FOR US

What goes into making us feel safe? On whatever path we're walking, into whatever experience we've never had before, what is the thing we reach toward to make us feel safe? At times it might feel like we should reach out to something close by, like Sam reaching for the mountainside. God tells us that our understanding of safety may be exactly the wrong thing. He tells us to trust him with our whole heart and *not to lean* to our own understanding. If we do that, if we learn to trust him, God is going to make the path work for us. I believe this is by instruction and conversation.

I used to think that it was by severe obedience. I thought that the only way to serve God was through obedience and that this was the most important thing to him, that rules were the most important thing to God. Through Jesus, I learned that the most important thing to God is us. Our obedience is not supposed to be as if we're tying marionette strings onto our limbs to be moved around by some puppet master in the sky. Jesus was commended for his obedience, but it was an obedience that grew out of a loving relationship, even a partnership. He was part of a partnership in recreating a loving relationship between God and the world.

In Phil 2:8, Jesus is recognized as humbling himself and becoming "obedient to death—even death on a cross." This obedience wasn't to God; it was to the objective. God the Father and God the Son and God the Spirit had the same objective: reuniting God with the world. This was obedience to what was required to clear away the death that had saturated souls. The objective was to kill death so it couldn't ever infect anyone again. We'll get into that later, but for now it is important to see that the word for "obedient" has a distinctly physical sense. It means to listen attentively and to respond positively (to what is heard). That's the experience of obedience. It can lead us into concepts like deference and submission, but first it creates a picture of relationship. God, Father, Son and Spirit, is a unity in relationships that seeks after relationship with us. Our image of God should include a relational experience of united effort that includes deep listening and responsive partnership.

When I listen to the person I love and respond positively to their words so that my actions reflect our relationship, I'm living out my love for them. In John 8:29, Jesus says,

> "The one who sent me is with me; he has not left me alone, for I always do what pleases him."

This depicts the relationship Jesus has with God but also the relationship we can have with God, that God is always with us and that we can hear God and respond to God. The Spirit of God is the one who surrounds us now and speaks into our spirits the guidance and directions that will allow us to "always do what pleases him."

When we think that following the rules is our primary responsibility, that makes things pretty cut and dry. Just learn the rules, and do the rules, and you'll be loved by God, and you'll get into heaven. Unfortunately, the responsibility not only cuts us off from a loving relationship but also leaves open this really human escape clause called "close enough." Most all of us respond, at some point or another, with a sense of "doing the best we can," and asking God to be satisfied with that. I watched and learned how people always had a good excuse for what they did that was questionable. I found that especially in myself.

Some of the Pharisees of Jesus' time were exquisite at this. Some of these particular religious leaders *knew without doubt* that the most important thing to God was obedience to the rules, so they became amazing rule keepers and makers. We should not fault them for seeking to be God's person, but some of the sect missed even that mark. Jesus called them out on that hypocrisy, because Jesus was calling them into a deeper relationship with God than what they felt they had to accomplish on their own.

Just one example of the way some Pharisees acted might make this clear. They understood that the Ten Commandments said that everyone should rest on the Sabbath. This was interpreted as a rule that meant "do no work." So, the discussion among people trying to keep all the rules arose over what work is. If we determine the limit of "work" when it starts, we'll be able to easily keep the rule that we shouldn't work on the Sabbath. As this discussion wound its way through many theories and arguments it was determined that work included walking too far. So, the phrase "a Sabbath day's journey" explained that one could walk only this far, and, beyond that, one was doing "work." But then the discussion went to . . .

"This far from where?"

"Well, from your home."

"But what if I'm not at home? What if I went to visit or to do business in Jericho?"

"Well, then it is your stuff. You brought stuff with you on your trip, so you can only go 'this far' from your stuff."

It wasn't too hard to come to the next step of realizing that if it was my "stuff" from which I could travel, then while on the way to Jericho, I could drop off a bit of "my stuff," every little distance that measured a "Sabbath day's journey," and so I could walk back to my home from Jericho (or wherever) and never be more than a Sabbath day's journey from my stuff ("home"). And I could do that even on the Sabbath and still be keeping all the rules. The importance of figuring all this out was to keep in relationship with God or at least to keep God from getting angry at me for breaking rules. If I kept the rules, then God loved me.

Doesn't this sound like the same kind of thought pattern as a teenager discussing a curfew with his or her parents?

"You need to be in by eleven."

"Okay, but what if, I, like, get in at 11:10 . . . am I in trouble?"

Parent, rolling eyes, "No . . . if you're in close to eleven, you're okay."

"So, like, 11:15 or so is still okay."

At this point, a parent should stop and say, "Oh wait . . . you think I'm talking about time, or maybe you think that I want to be in control of you. I'm not talking about time or control. I'm talking about love. I love you . . .

and I want you to be well, so I'm telling you I want you home so I know you're well and safe. Do you not think I love you?"

Did you ever wonder why Jesus got into such a deal with these types of people? And did you put together the problem within that question? Why would Jesus be breaking any rules if the rules are the most important thing to God? If some of the most exquisite rule makers and keepers had severe problems with Jesus, to the point of wanting to kill him, is there something about the rules that is wrong to Jesus? What was Jesus talking about that these people didn't understand? Were they talking about limitations and control when Jesus was talking about love?

In my Christian upbringing I learned that the divergence between Jesus and these Pharisees was because these kinds of Pharisees thought they would curry God's favor if they followed all the rules. Jesus was teaching them that it was God's grace that revealed his love. But then, I was told I needed to follow all the rules in order to be a good Christian. I was told I was not to lean to my own understanding but to God's understanding, and that meant God's understanding was summed up in the rules. Not leaning on my own understanding would be demonstrated by severe obedience to how my mentors interpreted God's rules.

And then one day I looked at those verses quoted above from Proverbs, while I was thinking about Jesus having problems with rules, and the words that stood out to me were *trust* and *understanding*. My trust was in my understanding of the obedience required of me and not in my relationship with God. So, I dug into the Hebrew behind this sentence and discovered that I should "acknowledge" God. Suddenly, I was not looking at a demand for obedience. I was being told that God had a greater understanding of the world than me and that I should learn his understanding. I should *acknowledge* God's way, that is, hear it and receive it, like wisdom. Walking in wisdom is different from walking in severe obedience. Wisdom grows out of relationship, authenticity and reality.

When the Bible refers to a person who does not acknowledge God it uses the word "fool." "A fool says in his heart, 'There is no God.'" (Ps 14:1) What would make a person foolish by not acknowledging God? It would be from not being able to see all there is to see in the world but still figuring I can handle it on my own. It's deciding that I don't need to believe in anything beyond my own capabilities and perception. A fool is someone who doesn't realize this is a silly way to live, a rather deceptive way to live. We act like we can take advantage of the world's resources and make them work for us, without realizing that our lives and whole selves will be diminished by doing that. The person who acknowledges God, God's reality, and God's understanding of reality becomes wise by partnering with the one who has the best perception of everything. That is different from believing in a set of rules or limits or a pattern of rituals. It suggests that there is a lot of the world that we do not understand, and we should be in relationship with the person who actually does understand it, who in fact knows it best.

The Bible tells on us to *fear the Lord* and that the fear of the Lord is the beginning of wisdom. This has nothing to do with being afraid of God because the fear of the Lord is, simply, humility. It is admitting I do not know everything. Clarity in that may not open the spiritual aspect of ourselves, but we are told there is nothing that works better.

For the Pharisees who had a problem with Jesus and for us, unfortunately, an approach of severe obedience also creates this "contract" with God, which essentially means "if I hold up my end of the bargain, you have to hold up yours." This can narrow down to "if I follow all the rules, stay within all the lines, regardless of how close I get to the far edge of the lines, you have to let me into heaven." (The teenager saying, "Then I'm still not in trouble, right!") You see, when Jesus was getting into trouble with the rule keepers, it was usually over things that demonstrated compassionate care of other people. Consider this example from Luke 13:10–17:

> On a Sabbath Jesus was teaching in one of the synagogues, and a woman was there who had been crippled by a spirit for eighteen years. She was bent over and could not straighten up at all. When Jesus saw her, he called her forward and said to her, "Woman, you are set free from your infirmity." Then he put his hands on her, and immediately she straightened up and praised God.
> Indignant because Jesus had healed on the Sabbath, the synagogue leader said to the people, "There are six days for work. So come and be healed on those days, not on the Sabbath."
> The Lord answered him, "You hypocrites! Doesn't each of you on the Sabbath untie your ox or donkey from the stall and lead it out to give it water? Then should not this woman, a daughter of Abraham, whom Satan has kept bound for eighteen long years, be set free on the Sabbath day from what bound her?"
> When he said this, all his opponents were humiliated, but the people were delighted with all the wonderful things he was doing.

This kind of moment also revealed that Jesus had a personal relationship of guidance between him and God, something much more than a contractual relationship with God. Seeing this anew made me wonder . . . what was God's understanding of *the rules* and obedience? Was God really the one who was telling us that we were despicable degenerates who weren't touchable or worthy of his love until we followed all his rules to the letter?

For so many years, people were told to crawl before the Holy God who demanded their obeisance. Now, let's admit right off that sometimes feeling "unworthy" can be completely appropriate. One of the words for "worship" in the Bible actually means "kiss," like when Jesus healed the blind man (John 9) and the man *worships* Jesus at the end of the story, like lying down to kiss. It is like *kiss the ground you walk on*. The image then is that this man, who can suddenly see for the first time in his life, falls before Jesus and kisses the ground before him. In such a moment, that is a reaction we can understand, just as we understand John Newton calling himself "a wretch" in his song "Amazing Grace." There are times when we can feel wretched and unworthy before God.

But what if that is not the relationship God has ever wanted with us. Jesus told us that when we feel like a wretched and unworthy child who returns to our father (especially after we treated him as worthless initially), claiming we have no right to be called his child and should just be used as a servant, the father is not hearing any of that. He throws a party (Luke 15) to welcome us back into the family. God wants to lead us into life, an abundant life, fully engaged and vibrant. Jesus also says that the child is celebrated as finally being able to see.

Is there something we aren't seeing, aren't celebrating, aren't engaged by when we keep thinking of God as demanding that rules be kept or that we should be his slave? In this story in Luke 15 of the prodigal, we are taught that the son who took his inheritance and left seemed to feel that he was an orphan. He told his father, "You're as good as dead to me." He and we learn, instead, that we had never been and never will be orphans. We have a creator who loves us.

And within this story we also are taught that we aren't slaves. There's an older son in the story. He tells the father that he has always obeyed and done everything he was told. He has slaved for the father. He is exasperated that the son who flaunted every command is given a party when he was never given one. The father, again, calls this son into relationship making clear to him that he owns everything . . . the party was his any time he decided to have one. Neither of these sons had ever seen the father as he was or lived in a loving relationship with him. Neither of them could see and so they could not hear his heart. It's when we finally see this that God and all that God has done and continues to do comes into focus. It's finally then that we can also hear.

I was on a mission trip to Haiti once, assisting a clinic and school in both construction and hygiene. I brought an eye doctor and a dentist along to aid people who might never get to one. The eye doctor brought donated glasses, and he was fitting them to people who had no money for glasses. One of them was a sixty-five-year-old man, and another was a seven-year-old boy. Their eyesight was so bad that neither had ever seen the world clearly. As the man received his glasses, seeing clearly for the first time, he began to cry. It took him a while simply to leave the room because everything was so vividly a part of him now. The doctor's face, his own hands, every aspect of the room was now something with which he was engaged. The man simply couldn't leave the room because every detail was so overwhelming. There was too much for him to take in, right in front of him. The boy had a similar experience, but it was outside. He left the room almost immediately, looking everywhere and at everything. There was so much to take in, and it was suddenly all clearly around him. Both were engaged with the life around them because they could participate in it.

Jesus came to re-explain God to us so we could see and hear clearly. If we look at the Bible as the history of people getting God wrong, Jesus comes to make clear to us what God was trying to get through to us since the beginning. But we did not see it. We couldn't hear it as he said it.

Another way to look at this might be like a misinterpreted email or text. Have you ever received a message that seemed like the person writing was angry or offended? You contact them, and they tell you, "No, no . . . I was saying it *this way* . . ." And they give you a different tone of voice to the words. Suddenly you see the words, hear the words, and you regain your relationship that you thought was torn. Jesus came to help us to see clearly but even more to hear clearly what God had been saying all along. Jesus is God's tone of voice.

We taught ourselves that God is tough and demanding and would lead us into purity . . . which we were all supposed to want more than anything. We also explained to ourselves that purity was something we could achieve by following all the rules. Perhaps we needed to be humble about it, continuing to temper our rule-keeping by saying we were never *really* pure. We kept saying that this was only with God's help, but that included mostly the work we had to do. (God just kept encouraging us with Bible verses we could memorize when it became hard.) And, if we messed up, God would forgive us. (That was his part of the contract, right?)

Jesus gave us a new understanding, as if he was telling us that we got God's tone of voice wrong. He didn't tell us a new thing. He taught us the old thing with a different tone of voice, the tone of voice that was within the words that we simply read and didn't hear. Jesus leads us to hearing as well as seeing, leaning into God's understanding, something we'll need to grow into throughout our lives, starting again each day.

I was brought up to know that things were much more cut and dry. You read your Bible, you get what it is saying, you do it, and God loves and rewards you for that. That was the point, and God was someone who likes things cut and dry because God loves rules most of all. I learned that God's sovereignty was like a king's sovereignty and that we were servants, *loved*, but servants . . . even slaves that were supposed to live in obedience.

I think we need to admit that many, many people like this. They like someone being in control because it provides a sense of security, which carries its own sense of control. If there is someone controlling life, then all I must do is line up within that environment of control and act the same way. We find this scattered in stories throughout the Bible. In a little bit, we'll look at how the people with Nehemiah (and some of those following) went for this in a big way. Even earlier, however, there was an attempt for control in Israel.

Back in the story of Samuel the Prophet we find that the people tried a different form of control. In 1 Sam 8:4–9, we read:

> So all the elders of Israel gathered together and came to Samuel at Ramah. They said to him, "You are old, and your sons do not follow your ways; now appoint a king to lead us, such as all the other nations have."
> But when they said, "Give us a king to lead us," this displeased Samuel; so he prayed to the Lord. And the Lord told him: "Listen to all that the people are saying to you; it is not you they have rejected, but they have rejected me as their king. As they have done from the day I brought them up out of Egypt until this day, forsaking me and serving other gods, so they are doing to you. Now listen to them; but warn them solemnly and let them know what the king who will reign over them will claim as his rights."

Straight along, the people wanted to find a means of control, seeking, even making, a god of control. And when things went wrong, and they tried to turn back to God, the people scolded themselves as being unworthy.

Instead of living into God's love, forgiveness and into the nature of living that God described to them, they tried to become better at keeping rules.

We need to re-look at the stories we've told ourselves while using the perspective of Jesus' explanation and example. God led us out of the orphanage and, as God told the Israelites, out of the house of slavery.

Chapter Two

When's a Command NOT a Command?

JESUS, AS THE TONE of voice of God, changes the experience of the Exodus and even the account of the Ten Commandments. The story we told ourselves is that after hundreds of years of domination and slavery, the people of Israel were led out into the desert to receive a list of commandments and a new position of slavery under a sovereign God.

Say anything you want about a loving and caring God in that moment, but the big THOU SHALT NOT. . . does not come across as anything but a command of a ruler to a servant or slave. But what if that was not how it was experienced. First off, there's the word "thou" that sounds so incredibly formal. When King James had his translators go at the process of producing an English version of the Bible, the word "thou" was the way everyone spoke to each other, regular people talking to regular people on the street, bumping into each other in the marketplace. The word "you" was used in formal situations, like before the king. So, the translators were telling the people who read their translation that God, the God of the Universe, spoke to the Israelites, like a friend, like a person in a shop. The first people who read the King James Bible heard it differently, and I'm suggesting that the first people who heard the Ten Commandments also heard them differently.

There's an old church sign that reads "It was Ten Commandments, not Ten Suggestions." It may not have been either. The people at the base of Mount Sinai received *instructions*. They were given understanding . . . what we call wisdom. The word we translate as "commandment" is also the word for "instruction." We chose to translate it as "commandment," but what if we translated it as "instruction"? What if God gave the people Ten

Instructions on how to live well, how to live well with each other and how to live well with God? Instead of hearing God securing his position above them, demanding obedience, we have God clarifying how people are to live with him and with each other in real life and speaking in a tone of voice that is friendly.

Scholars have taught us that the structure of the list of ten is like a *Suzerainty Covenant,* a contractual relationship that people were used to receiving at that time between a Suzerain, a ruler or king, and a people he conquered. Some have started arguing about that, but it gives us a form that was familiar with people of that time. Because of this, we have focused on the authority of a ruler rather than the relational experience of covenant between communities. The list of ten has a similar outline to a Suzerainty covenant, but it does not follow it exactly. One thing that is not usually brought up by scholars about this covenant is that the Suzerain expected the people to rule themselves. This suggests that there is something else going on within the covenant of God even if it followed a familiar format. It also points us back to compare this covenant with the earlier covenants in the history of the people of Israel. How did God express his relationship with people?

When God created a covenant with the man Abram, it was about a relationship, between the two of them (Gen 15) and the future generations of the people of Abram (Abraham). In that covenant, God showed Abram visually that he would not have to do any of the work of keeping this promise. God would do all the work. In the story, Abram has a dreamlike vision of a major sacrifice. A floating lamp appears on one side of the sacrificed animals, whose carcasses were split in half and laid down between the lamp and Abram. There was a path between the halves. This may seem a bit gruesome, but the word for making a covenant, literally, was "cut," one *cut* a covenant, and it was a matter of life and death. Lives were given up because it was so serious. The animals used in creating such a covenant were cut in two. At that time, as a covenant was made between peoples, the leaders sacrificed animals, laying the halved bodies of the slaughtered animals down on the ground in this way and then walking between them—one leader walking through from one side and then the other leader walking back through the same path.

As they then cut the covenant, the lifeblood (if not the gore) of the animals would get on each leader as they walked between the halves, and would speak to the serious level of relationship, that this relationship cost life. But, in this instance, in Abram's vision the lamp, representing God's presence, floats over to Abram's side and then, instead of Abram walking back to seal his part in the covenant, we're told that God sealed the deal. God takes on full responsibility to keep the relationship. This is at the beginning of the Bible in the section that we can see as history the way we think of history—with names, dates, and places noted. Here, toward the very beginning of the Bible, we read that God reached out to a human being to create a relationship by which the world would be blessed ("made happy or well-off" is the literal translation).

Instead of a life-building, happiness-based relationship, we taught ourselves that the new covenant at Sinai with the Israelites created ownership and control like a human does. We created a picture of God being like a big human being, like a king who demanded obedience so he could get what he wanted. We taught ourselves that God wasn't interested in having a sincerely joyful connection with us. He wanted to own us and force us into a restrained and systematically controlled life.

But what if the former slaves heard it with a different tone of voice? What if the Ten Instructions the people received were for living well as they live with God and other people in the world . . . but not with God controlling them as slaves.

We told ourselves that God hauled them out of four hundred years of slavery to demand control over them for himself. But if we read the words plainly, God came, and Moses keeps explaining, to bring about a relationship expressed as wisdom in how to live. In Deut 4:5–8 we read:

> I have taught you declarations and judgments as the Lord *my God instructed me, so that you may follow them in the land you are entering to take possession of it.* Observe them carefully, for this will show your wisdom and understanding to the nations, who will hear about all these declarations and say, "Surely this great nation is a wise and understanding people." What other nation is so great as to have their gods near them the way the Lord *our God is near us whenever we pray to him?* And what other nation is so great as to have such righteous decrees and instructions as this body of instructions I am setting before you today?

Check this with the translation you normally use and, if you can, the Hebrew behind it. Remember the word "commandment" can also be translated as "instruction." Also watch for "law," which is also translated as "guidance" in some places.

We chose to translate the word as "commandment" instead of "instruction." We chose to translate the word as "law" instead of "guidance." Thinking of these words with their alternative and yet legitimate translations is a shift in our understanding of God, and the essential change here, really, is to shift from picturing God as being like a big human, like an over-ruling king, to a being that is beyond us, not bigger or "up there" but filling everything, everywhere all at once—completely beyond us, and with an understanding that takes in everything faster than immediately, knowing it before it happens. We lean to his understanding because it is so beyond our ability to grasp and hang onto everything continually. We need to go back to both God and to God's guidance so we can see how it plays into any situation in which we find ourselves.

Does using the words *instruction* and *guidance* change the way the image of God hits your heart? Does it make you think of God differently? What would it mean if the people of Israel heard that God was releasing them into life and out of slavery? Would it sound like, "I have come that you may life and have it abundantly?"

Jesus is God's tone of voice.

Chapter Three

The Point Was Making Wise Choices That Produce Life

WISDOM IS A FUNNY thing. We all know it when we hear it, but even if we recognize it as wisdom, we don't always do it. Someone says "do your taxes early" or "change the filter in your heater," "do not overeat," and we think, "Oh, I should do that." Not too long ago I heard the advice that, "if you're going to rob someone's house, you should wear a mask." That was said in response to a video where someone was caught on camera breaking in without a mask. It's just wisdom. We recognize wisdom and tell ourselves, "That is a good idea. . ." and in a ton of cases that is as far as it gets . . . an idea. But wisdom is not a clever statement or a truth we design graphically so we can hang it on the wall. Wisdom is not wisdom until it is used. Wisdom is seen only in actions.

What if God was not looking for people obedient to rules as much as God wanted wise people in loving obedience to the objective of reconciling the world, people who were joining him in bringing life back to the people and the planet? Some people work so hard to be obedient to rules and worry over being good or pure, but what if wisdom was the point, acting wisely with God and others? That will broaden our understanding of what's involved in living. We aren't given a list of rules. We're given the helpful perspectives that speak into our own souls and speak to us about the souls around us, It provides us with guidance. Wisdom tends to be something we use when the circumstance we're facing is different than we thought, when we tried it on our own.

I was trying to start my lawnmower one day when a neighbor came by. We were chatting as I went through the process of getting a mower going that refused to work. As I was trying my fifth alternative he casually asked, "Did you check the gas?" When someone knows the necessity involved in making life work, their words are simply wisdom. I hadn't checked the gas, but as I was asked, I knew that was the problem. So, I checked and then went to get gas, filled the tank, and went to work.

God is speaking about the way we live in regular life and what is necessary to make it work as it was designed. God is telling us, in the Ten Instructions, how to be wise in seeking life, how to live life in a manner that works, in the way things are supposed to work. This changes the way we should think of obedience.

When we look at the commandments as "instructions," then God told the people at Sinai to dig into how to live rather than how to bow to his demands and to try to be perfect. There's been so much effort given toward becoming pure through obedience rather than alive and living well with God and each other, that it seems that Christians and other human beings have missed the point for a long time. Purity is an effort by humans to create a righteousness or even a sinlessness that is, already, a gift from God. It is like reaching out for something we believe will give us safety, something close at hand that we can lean on to give us security, that seems to make sense. Instead, living within and following God's wisdom is like knowing you will fall down the mountain if you lean to your own understanding and desire for safety, so choosing instead to hear and live within the heart of the instructions.

Being pure in heart is about integrity, being one thing internally, and acting in wisdom rather than being untainted spiritually. Integrity and being untainted point in different directions when they guide us in how to live. Having integrity speaks of an inner soundness that is carried into every area of life. When it is infused with God's Spirit and God's wisdom the relationship with the world is expanded. Being *untainted* means separation from anything that would challenge our purity. If Jesus' main purpose in coming was not to make us pure, to either "pay off" Satan or to "pay back" God (depending on how so many people look at the work of redemption), then his main purpose was *not* getting us into heaven but helping us to be alive fully with God and each other here and now. His main purpose was to see us grow into wholeness, both here and for heaven. Redemption was to clear out the presence of death in our souls, and forgiveness is about healing our souls instead of balancing accounts.

The Bible tells us that eternal life starts now for those who live well with Jesus. It is the natural, daily experience of living in God's wisdom. He actually meant it when he said, "I came that they may have life and have it abundantly," but he was not saying that would start once we get to heaven. We will look into living life now, and the impact of redemption and forgiveness a bit more later.

Discovering the list of ten as instructions rather than commandments teaches us that people have worked so desperately hard to become pure when what God was seeking is our wise and thorough involvement in living, joining him in creating a new society. This is the difference between integrity and trying to be untainted spiritually. Even if we have integrity, sometimes we are going to screw life up. There's too much we can't control in life, but God has given us a way of handling the moments when we mess up, and that's based on healing. It wasn't a transaction. We aren't supposed to try to pay God back for messing up. We are supposed to learn how we have an illness in our souls that needs treatment. It's not a malfunction as much as a deadening. That leads to finding a different type of solution.

We find it in living humbly with God and in understanding and kindness with each other. God was not seeking to separate us from the world, creating some manner of being "cleaner," more pure and holy. Instead, God gave us the tools and his presence to grow into a deeper engagement with him and with the world. God wants us to be in the world . . . "just not of it," not caught up in the ways people try to control it. He calls us out of being fools and out of our attempts to regulate life through our own understanding. Instead, he calls us into understanding how to live. God wants us to be with others in relationship even like in friendship with both people and God. Read this carefully. It's part of Jesus' prayer for his followers (John 17:14–19):

> I have given them your word and the world has hated them, for they are not of the world any more than I am of the world. My prayer is not that you take them out of the world but that you protect them from the evil one. They are not of the world, even as I am not of it. Sanctify them by the truth; your word is truth. As you sent me into the world, I have sent them into the world. For them I sanctify myself, that they too may be truly sanctified.

Jesus is praying that we will have God's presence and assistance within us, so we can live in the world as his people. We are "set apart," which is the meaning of "sanctify," which is also the idea of "made holy." We are to be different and sent into the world to be in relationship with others and with God. We aren't to be different like we're pure and they're not. We're supposed to be living in the wisdom of God, living a different way from the way human beings are used to others treating them.

The people at the foot of Sinai had just left demanding authoritarian rule of hundreds of years bearing down on them constantly . . . from other people. And we have told ourselves that God led the people out of that situation and into the desert, so that he could bring down even more of that through a new set of commandments. This perspective says that God brought the people out to the desert just to "jack up" the pressure on life. It could even suggest that God wanted the people to grovel before God more than their task masters in Egypt.

Authoritarian rule separates and isolates, emphasizing differences. This was not and is not the way of God. The overall message of the Bible, and what Jesus and the prophets in the Old Testament taught particularly, was that God calls people back into relationship. When God led the people out of slavery, from Egypt to the mountain, he did not bring them to new or greater demands in a new slavery, but to give them instructions on how to live differently as his people, with each other and with others around them. Coming out of slavery meant coming into life. Through that moment at Sinai, he gave us all his instructions so we could see how life works when it actually works well.

SO, WHY DID WE DECIDE THEY WERE COMMANDMENTS?

In the book of Nehemiah, the people of Israel return from exile. The Bible tells the story of king after king in Israel who led the people either toward or away from the love of God. There were seasons when a ruler brought about reform, but then things fell apart once again. Most of the time, a ruler wanted what they wanted when they wanted it. They were the king, and Samuel told them what kings would demand, and this sometimes meant they led the people into the worship of idols instead of God.

During this time, prophet after prophet kept calling the people back into relationship with the Lord, and we have their words recorded. They gave warnings to the people saying that the choices they were making were going to lead them so far away from God that God would just let them go finally. The prophets said the choices the people were making were breaking God's heart, and the results of these choices would bring about trauma and destruction. In Jer 9:1–3, we have an example of God's heartache:

> Oh, that my head were a spring of water
> and my eyes a fountain of tears!
> I would weep day and night
> for the slain of my people.
> Oh, that I had in the desert
> a lodging place for travelers,
> so that I might leave my people
> and go away from them;
> for they are all adulterers,
> a crowd of unfaithful people.
> "They make ready their tongue
> like a bow, to shoot lies;
> it is not by truth
> that they triumph in the land.
> They go from one sin to another;
> they do not acknowledge me,"
> declares the Lord.

And the trauma of exile from their land came as a result of them leaving God, "cheating" on God like a person committing adultery. Between the latest bullies on the block, the Assyrians and the Babylonians, the nation of Israel was taken apart, removing the leadership of the country and many of the people. The people of Israel went into exile. The prophets told them an exile was coming, but they also promised that a time would come when the people would return. In Jer 31, God tells the people they will return. He tells them to be ready to come back home again. In verse 21, God says:

> "Set up road signs;
> put up guideposts.
> Take note of the highway,
> the road that you take.
> Return, Virgin Israel,
> return to your towns.

And the people did return. Nehemiah, a Jewish man who was an official in the court of the Persians—the next bully who beat down Babylon—asked permission to go back to Israel and rebuild the city walls of Jerusalem. He got it, and this was part of the beginning of the return. As we read this heroic story that blends with the story of Ezra, a scribe and priest, we come to the time and place where the temple of God and the walls of the city of Jerusalem are rebuilt, and the people gather in celebration. You might say that Ezra had a macabre sense of timing. Instead of just a joyous celebration, at this moment, Ezra reads the words of God's law. A lot of people believe this was the book of Deuteronomy which contains the Ten Commandments like Exodus. The people hear the words, and scattered throughout the crowd are teachers who give them clarification. The people hear not only that these are the rules of God but that the reason they were exiled is because they broke the rules. They are ashamed of how their ancestors left God, and they recognize that shame is upon them as the descendants of those who didn't keep the law. They learn that, as a people, they were carrying the blame for this desertion of God.

So, the people made a promise, and at the end of chapter 9 in verse 38 of Nehemiah's story, we read:

> In view of all this, we are making a binding agreement, putting it
> in writing, and our leaders, our Levites and our priests are affixing
> their seals to it.

The people make a contract with God, literally promising they will never break God's rules again. Nehemiah is satisfied and goes back to Persia to report on how the rebuilding project has gone. When he returned to Jerusalem, however, he discovers that the people are already breaking all the rules again. Nehemiah kind of throws up his hands and asks God to at least remember him and how he tried.

Scholars tell us that it was at this time when the collecting, editing, and writing of what we call the Old or First Testament began. I am suggesting that the interpretation and emphasis on the rules and the use of "commandments" began at this moment. The people were taught and went on to teach to the next generations that the most important thing to God was the rules. If we break the rules of God, he hates us and his vengeance will come down on us, in the same way that we just experienced . . . being sent into exile. "We must never break another rule," became the intense demand, and if we neglect this demand, then every harsh event of nature or happenstance can be interpreted as God's severe punishment. Keeping rules removes us from God's heart, his love, and understanding. We end up just doing what we can, living the best way we're able, and doing it all on our own.

As you consider that, can you see that instead of *instructions* the people began to learn that these were *commands*? Instead of a God who understands the emotional state of his creation, who grasps the day-to-day issues that build up into lousy or demeaning or even horrific choices, who sees into the physical and mental breakdowns that lead us into addictive experiences . . . we began interpreting God's words and the life around us as revealing an angry, tempestuous God. We forgot the heartbroken words of a God who loves us, whom we hear of in the prophets and, instead, emphasized his anger, rather than seeing God in pain over being dismissed.

Not to say that God didn't get angry, but the prophets of God speak more clearly into a pathos or anguish of God than a ferocity. When we read the prophets who spoke to the people before they went into exile, they speak about God's heart being shredded by the choices and activities of the people with whom he desired to create a relationship that would change the world. The anger of God, the choice to allow his people to experience the full consequence of their decisions that were tantamount to their rejection of God, grew out of anguish.

This heartache is found throughout the Bible, even with the story of the first humans who are created to have a relationship with God, Adam and Eve. They deserted God's instructions on how to live and to find full lives. It's found in the demand of the people to Samuel, the prophet, to appoint a king, where God tells Samuel it is not his leadership they are rejecting but God's. And it is found in the New Testament, in the loneliest verse of the Gospels (John 6:66) where Jesus turns to his closest twelve disciples, after a host of his followers have turned away from him, to ask, "Will you also be leaving?" We have interpreted God's words as commands. They became, for many, a separating and divisive-from-communion declaration to the utter detriment of partnership and relationship with God in the world.

God is heartbroken when we leave him, forget his wisdom, and lean into our own understanding. Instead of seeking to love and to know God more deeply, however, we seem to have focused on God's anger. This seems to have all begun with the return of Israel after the exile and the creation of our Old Testament. It is not inappropriate, then, to look in the other direction as well, away from the history of Israel and into its future. From the last verses of Neh 9, the moment a contract was struck, we can mark the beginning of the way of relating to God that eventually created the sect of believers known as the Pharisees. And, as we've already considered, some of the Pharisees, who were so challenging to Jesus and the early Christians, were dedicated to the position of not breaking any rules.

These people became the torch bearers of the idol of purity. Because they thought they had a contract with God, they knew that God was required to provide them with heaven when they died. A famous story by Jesus reveals the arrogance and assurance of their position.
We read in Luke 18:

> To some who were confident of their own righteousness and looked down on everyone else, Jesus told this parable: "Two men went up to the temple to pray, one a Pharisee and the other a tax collector. The Pharisee stood by himself and prayed: 'God, I thank you that I am not like other people—robbers, evildoers, adulterers—or even like this tax collector. I fast twice a week and give a tenth of all I get.' "But the tax collector stood at a distance. He would not even look up to heaven, but beat his breast and said, 'God, have mercy on me, a sinner.' "I tell you that this man, rather than the other, went home justified before God. For all those who exalt themselves will be humbled, and those who humble themselves will be exalted."

Probably, the most famous Pharisee who became a Christ follower is Paul, the apostle. He reflected on his assurance in his letter to the Philippians (chapter 3) where he wrote:

> If someone else thinks they have reasons to put confidence in the flesh, I have more: circumcised on the eighth day, of the people of Israel, of the tribe of Benjamin, a Hebrew of Hebrews; in regard to the law, a Pharisee; as for zeal, persecuting the church; as for righteousness based on the law, faultless.
> But whatever were gains to me I now consider loss for the sake of Christ. What is more, I consider everything a loss because of the surpassing worth of knowing Christ Jesus my Lord, for whose sake I have lost all things. I consider them garbage, that I may gain Christ and be found in him, not having a righteousness of my own that comes from the law, but that which is through faith in Christ—the righteousness that comes from God on the basis of faith.

Paul refers to himself as "faultless" as a follower of the rules, but then shifts to his new understanding in Jesus. He says that in comparison to knowing Jesus and being known by Jesus, all he achieved in keeping the law was worth "garbage" . . . well, our four-letter-word for manure. We do not translate that straight in our Bibles, but that's what he says. He eventually understood that keeping rules was worthless and that God did not call us to be rule keepers, but wise followers and led by God's Spirit.

Paul's story is that he was blinded by God on his way to attack and arrest members of the Christian community. In his recovery, over the next few days, he came to believe fully in Jesus. He writes that after that he went away for three years. I believe it was during this time that Paul sat down with his own copy of the First Testament and re-read everything and, through the help of the Holy Spirit, came to a new understanding of God's heart and God's instructions. He came to see *grace*.

Chapter Four

Hearing

PAUL CAME TO THE place where he saw that the wisdom of God was different from the Law of God. In Rom 3:20–24, we read:

> Therefore no one will be declared righteous in God's sight by the works of the law; rather, through the law we become conscious of our sin. But now apart from the law the righteousness of God has been made known, to which the Law and the Prophets testify. This righteousness is given through faith in Jesus Christ to all who believe. There is no difference between Jew and Gentile, for all have sinned and fall short of the glory of God, and all are justified freely by his grace through the redemption that came by Christ Jesus.

We find the same thing as we take another look at the Ten Instructions. God was never demanding purity. This is clear from the start in the way God instructs the people at Sinai. Instead of boasting and lording it over the people, as happens in a human Suzerainty covenant, God says to them, simply, *I am Yahweh, your God, who brought you out of Egypt, out of the land of slavery* (Exod 20:1). What do you notice first here, ownership as a ruler or compassion as a savior? He even gives them his name.

The greatest aspect of God's authority is love and so God expresses Godself with compassion. "I brought you out of the pain of oppression." He has just led them out of everything they experienced in a destructive way of living with other people. These are people who had no memory of living another way and had almost no family histories of anyone living another way in several generations.

Then God lays out for them a new way of living. In Lev 18:3 we read:

> You must not do as they do in Egypt, where you used to live, and you must not do as they do in the land of Canaan, where I am bringing you. Do not follow their practices.

Instead of a new form of slavery, of subservience now to God, God calls the people into living well with God and with each other in wisdom. If we give up an overhanging cloud of "commands" and take on the clarity of *instructions*, we see clearly that we are being called to be wise rather than obedient to rules.

The word we translate as "obedient," as when Jesus is praised for being obedient (Phil 2:8), is literally "to give ear to" or "to be attentive." Jesus, it says, became attentive to God and God's way, even to the point of death, even to the point of death on a cross. With this understanding, the idea behind *obedience* is *partnership*. We join in, become attentive to, and respond positively to the wisdom of God and work with God in establishing God's dominion or realm. Our "obedience" is actually our submitting our opinions or perspective to partnership with God, God's way, and God's objective of loving the world. Another way of looking at this might be to think of a relationship with someone we love or on whom we depend.

When we enter into a relationship that is meaningful with another or with a group of others, we gradually shift our actions so that they reflect the nature and attitudes of that person or persons. This is why when your mom says, "That's not a good group for you to hang out with," it's probably true. As I wrote earlier, if we are in love with someone, we seek to act in a manner that reflects the importance of that person and that relationship. When we don't act in a way that reflects the relationship, we feel it. We can feel their disappointment even if they don't know what we've done. We seek to live in harmony with the inner emotions we have for them and with them.

In the best of relationships, this is a level of connection that isn't reflected in law or command. It reflects a living reality of love and joy and peace, all things we want to see grow ever more deeply within us. These three expressions of a true and loving relationship grow on their own. They are also the fruit that grows within our souls and characters, when the Holy Spirit takes up residence within us. (We'll look at this more thoroughly later.) This kind of obedience doesn't come from a demand or a regulation. It's more like a natural result of being in a relationship.

This is further reflected in the most important instruction that the Jews have held, as such, for centuries and that Jesus quotes when asked for it. It is found in Deut 6:4–9:

Hear, O Israel: The Lord our God, the Lord is one. Love the Lord
your God with all your heart and with all your soul and with all
your strength. These *instructions* that I give you today are to be
on your hearts. Impress them on your children. Talk about them
when you sit at home and when you walk along the road, when
you lie down and when you get up. Tie them as symbols on your
hands and bind them on your foreheads. Write them on the door-
frames of your houses and on your gates. (My italics highlight my
reinterpretation.)

In the Jewish community this is called the Shema. This title comes
from the first word of the verse in Hebrew—*shema.* It means "hear" and
some rabbis claim that this single word is actually most important—"hear,"
that is "to give attention to" or "to give ear to"—and that the people were
called on to *hear* within their hearts. If we still used the word "heed" it
would fit here. Loving God and living humbly in that love is the basis of
wisdom. It's seen in recognizing God's reality, seeking God's presence,
learning God's understanding in our full relationship with God, us hearing
God plainly and then following God's guidance. In Phil 2:5–11, we have
this beautiful description of the fullness of the relationship Jesus had with
God, that was expressed with his attentiveness to God, and his partnership
in the objective of God.

In your relationships with one another, have the same mindset as
Christ Jesus:
Who, being in very nature God,
did not consider equality with God something to be used to his
own advantage;
rather, he made himself nothing
by taking the very nature of a servant,
being made in human likeness.
And being found in appearance as a man,
he humbled himself
by becoming obedient to death—
even death on a cross!
Therefore God exalted him to the highest place
and gave him the name that is above every name,
that at the name of Jesus every knee should bow,
in heaven and on earth and under the earth,
and every tongue acknowledge that Jesus Christ is Lord,
to the glory of God the Father.

As we read the words "servant" and "obedient" and "becoming nothing," we might start to lean away from what I've lifted up about instructions, guidance, and wisdom. Isn't this speaking of severe obeisance? But what if the motivation was love and partnership? What if Jesus' attentiveness grew out of a loving partnership with God in how to care for the world? There is an extreme difference in the mindset of Jesus than with us. Right before this passage we read these words (Phil 2:1–4):

> Therefore if you have any encouragement from being united with Christ, if any comfort from his love, if any common sharing in the Spirit, if any tenderness and compassion, then make my joy complete by being like-minded, having the same love, being one in spirit and of one mind. Do nothing out of selfish ambition or vain conceit. Rather, in humility value others above yourselves, not looking to your own interests but each of you to the interests of the others.

This context clarifies the most dynamic difference. Jesus was in connection with God in a manner we find hard to imagine. Still, God has given us Jesus so that we will *hear* his tone of voice, so we can *hear* his heart and so we can learn from his example and imitate him. This imitation isn't created by our will power, but by the depth of connection, the relationship we have with God, and the depth of our partnership in God's objective. We can discover love for God, that opens us to the wisdom and the Spirit that will change us into Christlike beings.

It is important for us to understand what was going on in Jesus' life and death. Jesus was in partnership with God so that the people of our planet could be brought all the goodness of God's love. This is how and why he was obedient. It wasn't obedience to God. It was obedience to the objective, the obedience that was needed to accomplish the objective of revealing God's love to everyone. This is the partnership that God calls us into now, continuing the work of Jesus through the power of the Spirit. What Jesus reveals through his teaching and his dying is an authority that grows from authenticity in relationship. This authenticity is from the love and humility and partnership he had in relationship with God.

We need to hear this as we consider the experience of the Israelites coming out of slavery. At Sinai, we do not find an authoritarian ruler, like some bigger human being, who demands allegiance. This doesn't carry authenticity in our world or in God's way. God is the one who loves us best and who is showing us the truth, the deeper authority of love and community.

It is because of the authenticity of God's love for us that we become ready to give God our hearts and become passionate through his Spirit's work within us to join with God as partners. This is the way the world works and the way the world will work best.

The guidance of God, based in relationships, is not like rules. It is an expression of truth like gravity in physics. It never goes away and is part of how the world is created. Just like following the nature of gravity leads us into the ability to fly, recognizing the wisdom of living with God leads us into seeing the instructions that lead us into wholeness, into health, and well-being in ourselves and with others. God's instructions lead us into partnership with God in creating life filled with well-being for ourselves and everyone else. This is what I believe Paul discovered in his time away from everything and everyone. He discovered that the most important thing to God wasn't rules or keeping rules but that the instructions were given so we could find life and find God.

Chapter Five

Considering the Worth of the Instructions

WE NEED TO REREAD the instructions God gave the Hebrews in Exod 20. We need to seek to hear them with a different tone of voice than many of us have heard them. We need to hear them as coming from someone who loves us, who knows us, and who understands how life works. These words are the basis of expressing God's grace to the world. They are guidelines for how human beings will live well together. Other people may choose to live without this wisdom but not us. These will help us to see into the heart of God and to find God's love for every person on the planet. Fundamentally, they're about giving up control and making life work for everyone, rather than just us.

God tells the people, first, not to put some other power or authority in his face, to know him first as the God who loves them enough to save them. He says:

> You will not have any gods before me. (Ex 20:3)

The literal words here mean "do not put other gods in my face."

He tells them that there is nothing else. Do not go off seeking some other power. This is because the powers we find or create focus on giving us what we want, when we want it and not on participating in the world. They seek to keep us immature, rather than participating in the world. They are determined to own us, rather than to free us to participate in the world.

Finding any other god is really the beginning of seeking control and coming under control.

God tells them not to treat him the way gods are created by the people around them, created by their own hands as an attempt at control, placating one or another god to get what the people want, to get their own way. Instead of seeing God as magic, something that will change our circumstance immediately, God leads the people to realize that God works to heal destructive relationships within a handful of generations and that his love works in real time in the way we were created. He works with real healing that doesn't intrude on or manipulate unnaturally the personality of an individual. Look for this in this next instruction:

> Do not make for yourself an image in the form of anything in heaven above or on the earth beneath or in the waters below. Do not bow down to them or worship them; for I, the Lord your God, am a jealous God, visiting the depravity of the parents to the third and fourth generation of children of those who hate me, but showing love to a thousand generations of those who love me and observe my instructions. (20:4–6)

If you check this with your Bible, you may see that I chose the word *depravity* where some texts use the word "sin." It's the same word in Hebrew. If God's work is moving in a pattern that is natural to how life works then, he is going to lead people back toward him. This is telling the people that God is the one who brought them into a freedom of living, and they should not go looking toward other gods that will demand destructive obedience for fast results. And if they do, God promises that he is going to work against these acts of control. These gods will start by making us believe that we are getting some control over the world, but they move us into a required obedience that demands more and more of us. God's love will work against these man-made objects and attitudes in the same way that gravity works against our structures, weakening them until they fall.

In this instruction, it seems that God promises to be the one who breaks down destructive practices by the third or fourth generation of a family. The people of Israel just left a demanding control over their lives, and God is not leading them into his control or domination but into wisdom. More than that, he is letting them know that if they seek control over life, then the destruction and slavery that will inevitably follow that choice will be broken down by God himself. God is working to free all of us from everything that would demand control over us.

31

We may believe that we are not dealing with idols anymore, but idols don't have to be little statues or images. The power of an idol isn't in its representation. It is in the control we believe it might have over life and the control we believe it might give us in handling the issues of life. Think of the depraved or destructive ways people attempt to control life, feelings, experiences, or even other people around them. They choose opioids, pornography, anger, abuse, power, armed attacks, emotional manipulation, overwork, or even personal authority in an area. All of these can become attempts at controlling life. We create these gods which become idols from whom we demand power to make the world work the way we want it to work. We demand that they make us feel better, stronger, more relaxed, oblivious or in charge, but then these gods take control of us. The more we use them, the more control they have over us until we worship them. We become dependent on them to get us through life. God makes plain that life is not about control, because he does not want to see us be controlled or seeking control.

Then, in the second instruction, God says not to misuse his name. People at that time believed that if you could obtain a god's name you could control a god:

> Do not misuse the name of the Lord your God, for the Lord will
> not hold anyone guiltless who misuses his name. (20:7)

God is telling these people over and over that they are not to look toward control but relationship. So, God leads them away from the tools of "safety" that look so inviting. "Stop leaning toward the mountain and listen to me." They learned that God is not afraid of them learning God's name. He gives it to them immediately. He is not afraid because his name does not control him. It creates a means of communication. It is personal, engaging their emotions and sense of intimacy. God calls them into this nearness just as he called Moses to come close to the burning bush and to take off his shoes.

Breaking these first three instructions down then, God tells the people not to look to any other authority for guidance or strength and that they should not try to use God or have authority over God. God tells the people not to seek any other power of control over life, to stay and grow with him and to know him through what he does, and that is to bring healing to the world, and not to try to turn their relationship with God into *magic* by trying to use God's name or any other means including "severe obedience" to control God (v. 7). Life is not about controlling. It is about living within the interdependent nature of relationships in the world.

WHEN WISDOM BECOMES THE WAY LIFE WORKS . . .

Continue to look at the first three instructions and let's walk through them again.

God tells us to focus on being in an authentic relationship with him, living life as it comes, and that we shouldn't and won't find control in something around us, especially in something we create ourselves. Seeking after control by creating something we believe will deliver it rejects the one who loves us best and the depth of relationship we can have with this person. But if we do choose something other than freedom, whether it is in creating an idol like a statue or an idol like a dominating activity or substance, God promises not to let those things stand. God is jealous regarding his role in our lives because no one else understands life as God does. God loves us. God will not let stand a thing that separates us. Alcohol, drugs, sexuality, overwork, eating, romance novels, scrolling the internet, anything that captures our attention or devotion or that demands that we placate ourselves by using it, will come up against God's guidance. These are things that will punish us ultimately by securing a place in our homes or in our minds or in our hearts or in our bodies. God will work against anything like this until someone hears and responds to his love and call.

The word translated in these verses sometimes as "punish" is actually "visit." The ideas and vast differences between "punishment" and "visiting" are seen in the impact of choices that carry on generationally. We are choosing to say that God damages people and their lives when they make unwise choices, as opposed to saying that God recognizes the presence of something that is damaging in someone's life and begins to work against it.

The difference between these two ideas is either experiencing this as a living reality of anger lashing out against us, or as the natural outcome of poor choices or even horrible practices in life that live in our lives for a while. God is not telling the Israelites, nor us, that he is going to exact destruction on us for breaking rules and will continue that destruction for a handful of generations. God is letting us know the effect of our choices on our families and in our communities when we separate ourselves from loving God or others by seeking control and how God will respond to that.

God works in a natural manner that fits with the nature of our world, the nature of how we are created.

Like falling because of gravity, God is explaining to them and us the consequence of damage resulting from addiction, corruption, abuse, all and any attempts at seeking control over life or others. Attempts for control become idols, things we create for ourselves, but under whose demands we will eventually serve. Unfortunately, the damage of this is imitated by (if not just inflicted on) one generation to the next for at least a few. It will have a lasting impact that God hates because it blocks our experience of his love for us.

When we claim that this passage is speaking about some retribution by God, suggesting that God will *punish* for three to four generations, we further separate ourselves from God and each other. In our minds, God now rises far above us, uncaring about our issues or heartaches except to damage us further. Along with losing any sense of our own relationship with God, this can also move us to blame, shun, or reject other people whom we believe are receiving retribution. We can see lousy choices in their lives and the consequences that follow as God's anger or hatred of them. And when we believe we are not receiving retribution like they are, obviously, then we can see ourselves as better "rule keepers." God loves us more than them because we're "good" and they're not.

But if God is instructing us in how life works, then God is telling us that the consequences of our choices will have an enormous impact, even onto grandchildren and great-grandchildren, then we see it as the *visitation* of this destructive reality. When it lives with us (*visiting*) as the consequence of our choice, we realize that the consequences continue until someone says, "I am not living with that anymore." Even if it takes three or four generations down the way, someone says to themselves, "why are we doing this?" Or "that's it. . . I am done! No more! I am out of here!" And then they begin to make other choices, to live in a new way.

What causes the change?

I have no doubt that God is involved with every person, every heart and spirit on the planet. So, suppose God's Spirit finally gets through to someone, after working for generations, until it reaches that one and they started listening to God's Spirit within them again. Maybe they don't even recognize it as God, just a sense of being fed up with all the chaos or damage in their lives. People don't have to recognize God's hand in their lives for it to be active. Regardless of whether they attribute the shift to God's guidance or not, the Spirit works past the damage caused by a parent or grandparent or great-grandparent's depravity and leads a new generation back toward life. These verses are telling us that God is continually at work with everyone, seeking to reach every person in the world. They are telling us that God is a jealous God, someone who loves us, everyone, and doesn't want to share that relationship with someone or something else, especially something that dominates us and removes us from him. So, God is going to work against anything that separates us from him, that takes up residence in our lives, even if it takes generations to get people to see and join him in reacting against the damage.

It is not inappropriate for us to see this as the work of God's Spirit in every person in the world. Why would we think that God is not involved with everyone, anyone? The Holy Spirit is the complete and continual presence of God at work to bring healing into the world, to draw the whole world back into relationship. So, through a natural recovery process, moving out of trauma, the Spirit breathes into the souls of those impacted by the damage done by sin who are aching to be free. God leads human beings back toward well-being, toward the fullness of relationship and life. This is how the jealousy of God is expressed. If we miss this love for us, we can think that the work of reconciliation is all on us.

Happily, a man told me one day how his sister had come to faith finally. She had been rebellious in her lifestyle and left the faith as a young person, he said. "I've been praying for this for twenty-five years, and God finally answered my prayers." I thought that was curious and responded, "I'm so grateful and glad to hear this, but, you know, I bet God answered that prayer the first time you prayed it."

"What do you mean?" he asked.

"I bet, when you prayed for your sister the first time," I said, "and asked God to speak into your sister's heart, to bring her back into relationship, that God immediately said, 'Yeah! We're already working on that!' And God's Spirit talked to her spirit, pointed out things in her path, gave her encouragements to track new understanding, walked her out of damage in her life and heart until she saw God's love plainly and came to faith 'naturally.' It just took twenty-five years for her to get there."

He looked at me for just a moment and then said, "No . . . no . . . it was my twenty-five years of praying that did it."

Do you hear the need for control in that comment? Do you hear the contractual way of living in that comment? Do you hear the "magic" expected in that comment? Control over or a contract with God suggests a god who has no interest in healing and wants only obedience, and responds with "magic" when obedience is kept. This is not partnership with God. It is not being attentive to the heart and voice of God. This is a god we have to badger until he gets so bugged that he does what we ask. Jesus told a parable about this, revealing the nature of God in Luke 18:2–8:

> He said: "In a certain town there was a judge who neither feared God nor cared what people thought. And there was a widow in that town who kept coming to him with the plea, 'Grant me justice against my adversary.'
> "For some time he refused. But finally he said to himself, 'Even though I don't fear God or care what people think, yet because this widow keeps bothering me, I will see that she gets justice, so that she won't eventually come and attack me!'"
> And the Lord said, "Listen to what the unjust judge says. And will not God bring about justice for his chosen ones, who cry out to him day and night? Will he keep putting them off? I tell you, he will see that they get justice, and quickly. However, when the Son of Man comes, will he find faith on the earth?"

If we imagine God as controlling, even as desiring control, as rejecting or destroying those he does not control, we are living with an image of God that is just a big human being. We miss the God who is compassionate, wise, life-giving, and intimately engaged with the entire world and beyond us in every way.

Do you wonder if this is God's nature as you read the Bible? Think of God being truly God and involved in every moment, every aspect of the living planet, not controlling it but engaged with it. Imagine that God is engaged in bringing life into every seedling, movement into every heartbeat, healing into every catastrophe. There is a natural order to weather and climate and if we learn it, we learn how to live in it, but we also see that it moves into healing after it has been damaged. Or consider simply, how God has created humanity.

God created us so that we would heal. More than just physically, God tells the people at Sinai in this instruction that God works to heal us relationally. We see, revealed in the expansion of this third instruction, the depth of God's participation in all of life. Over and over God is telling us that God is involved with everyone. God loves everyone. Not loving or even knowing God does not stop God's love. Rejecting or not admitting God's presence does not stop God's love. Nothing stops God's love toward any and every person.

God's involvement in healing the world, reaching out to everyone and every part is seen in the way all of us are created. Healing is God's work, built within human beings. A doctor cannot produce healing. The doctor's job is to discover what blocks natural healing from taking place and then to clear it away, to let the process take place. Every part of us that mends itself demonstrates it, even deep within our psyches.

Consider the "grieving process" human beings go through that's been described by various doctors. They did not invent the process of grieving. They observed regular features, activities, processes and have spent years seeking to explain it, but, essentially, they discovered it, like the Norsemen found America. It was always there. They just came upon it. The grieving process was created within us so that we might heal. As we move through the experience of grief because of trauma that has come upon us, we have an ability to move from pain and detachment to re-engagement with life. Not to say we can't get stuck in grief, even wallow in it for the rest of our lives, but God does not want us to live within trauma. God does not want to see us separated and left in despair. God built within us the process to move through it and back into life and into what is life-giving. God gave this to every human being, not just those who worship him with knowledge.

The God Jesus explained and demonstrated to us is one who came seeking every person on the planet, who sends the weather on and for every person. In Matt 5:45 we read:

> He causes his sun to rise on the evil and the good, and sends rain
> on the righteous and the unrighteous.

God loves those who love him and those who don't. He's the one who knows how many hairs are on the head of every person. Every person is precious to him. This is the understanding of life the instructions of God call us to live out. There is a passage in Scripture that seems to speak against this. In Rom 9 we read that there are "vessels of wrath" as well as "vessels of mercy." When we read these words, we expect them to mean that God creates some people for destruction and some for preservation. But the active and passive language in each of these is important. In Greek, the people who are "vessels of mercy," those receiving mercy are fitted to hear mercy. The Greek is an active tense. God is helping them to be ready. They are prepared for mercy. The "vessels of wrath" are able to move into wrath. It is a passive voice in that God doesn't make them that way, but life can prepare them for destruction. It says that God bears with great patience those who prepare themselves for destruction, in order to show his true nature to those who he is preparing for mercy. Throughout Scriptures we're shown that people choose to harden their hearts by walking away from God.

INSTRUCTIONS ON HOW TO LIVE WITH EACH OTHER

As we move through the rest of the instructions of God, we come to number four in Exod 20:8–11.

> Remember the Sabbath day by keeping it holy. Six days you shall labor and do all your work, but the seventh day is a sabbath to the Lord your God. On it you shall not do any work, neither you, nor your son or daughter, nor your male or female servant, nor your animals, nor any foreigner residing in your towns. For in six days the Lord made the heavens and the earth, the sea, and all that is in them, but he rested on the seventh day. Therefore, the Lord blessed the Sabbath day and made it holy.

Some people believe the first four *commandments* are about our relationship with God. I am suggesting that the whole set of instructions is about giving up control and living with God and other people wisely. So, in instruction four, God tells the people how to live with each other as well as in relationship with him, and the first thing God says is "do not overuse yourselves or anyone else." This instruction is also the clearest demonstration that God did not pull the enslaved Israelites out of Egypt just to enslave them again.

The fourth instruction is "take a break!" God's guidance on living with others and him is to live exactly the opposite of how they have been living as slaves. This expression of Godself and God's understanding of humanity brings the instructions into clarity.

This instruction pronounces inherently . . . I love you! I am for you! Give yourselves a break! Take a deep breath. Everyone! Everything! Take a whole day every week and kick back, enjoy each other, learn each other, discover how the world looks through different eyes, and make sure that everything and everyone around you does the same thing, even your servants, even your animals, and even that guy who's just passing through. Invite him to take a break with you. This is the way I am, God says. This is the way you should be.

The depth and importance of this instruction on living with each other by first fitting in rest cannot be overstated because it reveals the nature of God to us. God reveals God's heart by making a piece of time *holy*. Something we can never touch, gold-plate, set up on a shelf or put into its own room, so we can show everyone that, "This is HOLY." The very first thing made holy is a chunk of time (Gen 2:3) and God says, this is how you mark holiness . . . it becomes special by being used differently, by giving yourself to it, and by seeing that it does not require anything of you. It is easily shared. Everyone gets in on it and it builds you up, builds the community up and it gets you thinking about what is deeply important in the richness of life. It's just set apart as different from the rest, which is the main idea of "holy," set apart as different.

The thing that is different about God's holiness from ours is that it is simply separated from the way other things like it are. It's also *special* in that is fills us with life and involves others. It is not made to make us pure, the way we practice purity. It is different because it becomes the basis of everything else we do, and it becomes different by how we participate in it, fully. This suggests that God's way into holiness is to enjoy this difference, this special nature, as interwoven and relating with God and the rest of life. So relish it and relax with everyone and everything around you.

The rest of the instructions are focused on remembering the worth of other people and not using others as tools for our own satisfaction or gain. Jesus gets into them in his Sermon on the Mount, which we will look at in a little bit. It's there that he makes clear the depth of these instructions. Living life with commandments is about rules, keeping or breaking them. Living life with God's instructions is about being wise instead of foolish. Remember, foolishness in the Bible is not about lacking common sense. It is living as if God is not a part of life, not real. It is also living as if others have no worth or, at least, not as much worth as I have. When we focus on trying not to break "rules" our relationships become artificial, just organized, controlling structures. God is not with us. We are just trying to achieve control through our own efforts. We are allowing our fears to control us. We are trying to lean onto the mountain for safety, even though we are putting ourselves into the gravest danger.

Chapter Six

Wisdom is Not Control
And, Also, Not Seeking Control

FOLLOWING COMMANDMENTS MOVES US toward an attempted control of life from which God is trying to lead us. Along with seeking power that replaces God, it allows us to lord it over other people as if we are better at keeping the rules than they are. It can lead us into judging which sins are worse than others while, perhaps, excusing our own sins. In the other direction, it can also allow us to condemn ourselves and even convince ourselves that there is no way God could love us. We become the decision makers instead of partners with God, and it separates us from others and from the world.

This can help us to realize, even more deeply, that when Jesus gives us his instruction to *love each other*, it is more than a practice that represents our relationship with him. It reflects the instructions God gave Moses and the Hebrews at Sinai. God's instructions draw us to each other, seeing the needs we share while recognizing the worth of each other.

When we think of control, we can think that God is the one who makes everything happen. But God is not the one who "gives and takes away." That is how Job thought of God (Job 1:21) when his story begins. By the end of Job's story, we discover that Job got God wrong. He discovers that God works a different way. Throughout the story Job gets all his arguments lined up after he has defended himself to his friends. He's been a great rule keeper. He is so good, that now, at the closing of the story, he is ready to defend himself to God. He is faultless, pure, he believes. Look at all the good he has done. How could God possibly treat him this way? "I am good! So, now God has to keep up his end of the contract and accept me, or at least give me a good explanation on why these tragedies of life are happening to me."

This contractual relationship is a level of control that replaces God and our connection with God. We're told that damage or destruction comes upon us because we've gotten God angry with us. That's a lot of what Job's friends tell him. But we can also find people who know that God is "in control," who tell us that although we may be good, God is doing something through the destruction that's been brought down on us. We hear people tell us that "God has a plan," or "this is just the way God needed it to be," or "we can't always understand God's designs," or "We just need to have faith." When we hear those things, we're being told that God controls everything, and whatever is going on is something that God planned. God asked Job to explain goats or does or wild donkeys or ostriches or . . . other parts of the natural world and why they live and act as they do. He asks Job to explain how the world works as it is, as it has been created. Job can't. Job can't see everything. So, he covers his mouth and apologizes to God.

I worked with a community in Uganda at one point. The church I was with at that point, helped them build a preschool and then a school system (up to twelfth grade). Our church had been brought in touch with this community through an internet search by a young woman there. She had been diagnosed with a hole in her heart. She searched for a surgeon who might help her since there were none in Uganda. Online, she found a surgeon who was a member of our church, and this woman said she would help the young woman from Uganda with an operation. The relationship with our church began. She and her uncle were brought to our community and received a successful operation. Some time later, when we were working with the village to create the larger school, someone told the young woman, in front of me, that the hole in her heart was put there by God, so that good things could happen to the village. What a horrible thing to consider. I spoke with her afterwards to tell her that this isn't the way God works. God doesn't damage us to make good things happen. God uses the damage of our lives to prepare us to discover mercy, if we're open to see it. She was ready to see it that way.

Some people aren't. Some people want an explanation that will make them feel secure in their assurance or knowledge of how the world works. They push away a God who works as God, in whatever way he desires, and accept a god who works in the way they want him to work. They want a god who works tit for tat, who gives and takes away, who is explainable, rather than a God who is beyond us and is not only working with us individually, but also working with the whole universe, every aspect of life, and fitting it all together as we move through it.

But does this mean that there is a plan and it is just hidden? Suppose it doesn't. Suppose it suggests that there is a created nature to life, and it can be used wrongly. We can claim that God has a plan for everything, rather than that God created everything with a nature we must seek to understand before we attempt to use it. And, also, that God will bring good out of anything, for those who hear him, receive him, and follow him.

We try to make sense of randomness, especially random acts of violence, by suggesting that God had to have it happen for some unknown reason. Do you know why the seven-year-old gets senselessly shot and killed on the front porch of her house in the inner city? It is because she happened to be on the porch when the car full of people seeking control over life with weapons unloaded them.

God did not plan that. God is not controlling life that way. "God's in control" is a lie. This is what Job discovered. God designed the world, and we can take the time to discover how to be part of it, or we can try to control it, or we can pretend that we have control. It's when we demand control that we unleash destruction on ourselves and on others. It's as we learn the nature of the world and work with God in it that we discover grace and protection.

There's a story about two houses surviving devastating catastrophes. In one year, a hurricane swept into Florida at about the same time wildfires were lighting up southern California. Someone noticed that the reporters were giving their news reports in front of the devastation across the country from each other, but in the background, there was a single house still standing, beyond the destruction behind the reporters, one in Florida and one in California. The single house gave a good background, and that's why the reporters stationed themselves there. The standing houses broke up the images of the devastated landscapes. Finally, someone wondered about that. Why were those houses still standing in both places, surrounded by devastation? A reporter went to the owners of each of the houses and asked why their house was still there, finally. The owners gave similar stories. They had built their house in a place where they hadn't lived before. They went to the state and asked for guidance and were told, respectively, about hurricanes or wildfires that happened in that area. They built their homes according to the state's guidance and instructions. If we don't demand control but learn how nature works and live (or build) in line with it, we survive. This is the world God has made. We can demand that it bend to our will, or we can seek to live as creatures who share in its nature. We can live as participants and partners, or we can try to be owners.

GIVING UP CONTROL MEANS LIVING IN RELATIONSHIP WITH GOD AND OTHERS

It's hard to give up control, and it is hard to give up the idea of God controlling everything. One of the issues people face regularly as believers is the reality of evil, in particular the suffering of the innocent, when we trust in God. When we make God's highest priorities rules and purity, we make control a feature of God. We suggest that God demands things work a certain way, that he has a plan or structure that can't be thwarted, but then we live in a world that denies that constantly. We have attributed this to a connection between "original sin" and the devil, suggesting that it is because Adam and Eve ate the apple, and saying, now, that we're living in a world separated from God. We'll get into the nature of sin later, but we tell ourselves that the chief thing that the first people created to have a relationship with God did was to break a rule. This made God furious with them and he cursed them, denied them the paradise in which they had been living and banished them from his presence.

What if God was telling them that they have walked away from him and left their relationship with him by seeking to control life? What if those who were to have a relationship and partnership with God didn't break a rule but broke God's heart? What if the curse was the natural result of choosing separation, rather than a hex or spell put upon them? They unleashed death into their souls. This isn't just physical death but spiritual death. This is the experience within us when we live against our relationship with God. It is death. Something inside us dies, something that should be working.

The result of this death is how it impacts our relationships with other people, with God, and with the rest of creation. We are cut off, not because a rule was broken but because we are deadened to our own responsibility for and interdependence with each other and the world. We blame God, we challenge God, we dismiss God because of our own evaluation of how the world should work. We then throw our effort into gaining control over life and over others. Or we dismiss control completely where anything can be fine. We decide that there is no way to have control, and so we give ourselves over to believing that anyone's "truth" has the same value as anyone else's "truth." And then truth disappears, as does God. We don't seek a partnership, a seeing and hearing of God's voice in ourselves or through the design of the world. We expect that God is not interested, not worth the time, or is non-existent.

Something we keep missing in our consideration of this is our own personal effect on the world. We set aside all the power within ourselves because of the deadening of our sensitivity to how the world works. We have the power to create parties that celebrate our cooperation with each other, with the natural world and with God. We have been given all authority over the world and can either shape it, demand that it allows us to control it, or we can work with it. We ask "where is God?" at moments of tornadoes or monsoons or earthquakes or random violence. We demand that our elected officials come up with answers. We don't spend as much time recognizing our own power and responsibility.

It may be that we struggle with that because we think we must come up with the biggest answers, rather than simply doing what we can with what's in front of us and learning how life actually works. A lesson in not seeking control but seeking partnership with God can be found in the story of Spirit Lake, near Mount St. Helens in Washington State. After the volcano erupted and blew the top off the mountain, the lake and its environs were decimated. The lake itself was filled with debris and ash. There was a move to rectify the damage, to clean it out and to try to bring it back to life, but an alternative idea was suggested. The idea was to wait, to see how healing took place naturally. Within a few years the lake moved back to health. The land around it still carries the scars of the volcanic holocaust, but it is coming back as well. We can see what happens when we don't immediately move in with our best guesses and try to control a situation. Healing is built into our system, our nature, and the world's nature. Wisdom is learning how life works and then partnering with it.

The difference between instructions and commands, then, is the difference between wisdom and a spreadsheet. One is about discovering and living in collaboration with life as it is experienced, and the other is about calculating and quantifying life's experiences to get a result. This is the nature of the choice offered to us, either to live in relationship with the living

God, with other people and in relationship with the rest of God's creation, or to bow down to a thing we created that demands we fill in and line up our columns correctly.

God's instructions and God's relationship with us are given to engage us with life and living with others. It might be better to think of God's way as being *in charge*, rather than God seeking control. Because God loves us and understands the possibilities of every choice or action, ultimately, everything will work out the way God wants it to work out. Instead of God controlling every detail of life, we realize that life will continue to work according to the nature of how it was created. God, in response to the separation we create from him and the nature of the world, works intimately within us to draw us back into wholeness, to living fully with him and the rest of creation. The instructions, then, are about making sure we do not lose touch with the importance of God, or the importance of ourselves or the importance of the person next door or the importance of the nature of creation. They are about how the world works best. Life becomes full and abundant because we are living in relationship with God and with others. These two have become most important to us (Mark 12:28–34).

IS THE WRATH OR THE FEAR OF THE LORD THE BEGINNING OF WISDOM?

Screwing up the instructions of God then does not get us into trouble like breaking a rule, like God's going to yellow or red card us and penalize or kick us out of the game. Rejecting the instructions of God messes up life for real. It messes up other people and their lives along with our own. It messes up the world. Messing up on the instructions kills something that is supposed to be working inside us; it kills something that should be part of the nature of the world. It kills, sometimes, other people.

This talks to our hearts about God's control versus God's authority. As I wrote before, God's authority is love with the authenticity of gravity, nothing escapes it. This is different from control. God's engagement with our world is not like the styles of control we might imagine if God were just an over-sized human being with superpowers. Human beings try to create order, to demand structures, objectives, and controlled outcomes. The problem with this is our limitations. We can only see so far. That's why our solutions all work, but only for a while. God, on the other hand, knows the outcome of every possibility. God knows what can happen to us as we reject his love for us and others. But God has no trouble engaging any choice to move its consequences into the direction he wants life to move ultimately.

This challenges our idea of the wrath of God coming down on someone and slamming them into submission. We can wonder, especially as we consider the history of our world, "why didn't God stop something or change something?" If we believe in the wrath of God, why don't we see it when things in the world are clearly filled with destruction? In the next chapter we will consider the wrath of God in depth, but here we need to be clear that we do not "fear the Lord" because of his wrath. God's wrath is not directed at us. God's wrath is toward what separates us from him.

That suggests a couple of things. We have the tools in our hands, the instructions that will keep us from allowing the tragedies that fill our history. We can choose to disappoint God, even to spit in his face and choose our own direction and control. We can even claim that "God's on our side" or that God wants the destruction we are bringing down on someone else or even see coming down on us as we seek control. Or, as we walk in wisdom with others, we can learn that God will continue to work toward restoring the world regardless of our decision to reject it and work against it.

God wants us, that is everyone, to live and breathe freely and to lead others into living and breathing freely. Rejecting the instructions of God then leaves us without the breath we need, living within the wrath of God. The wrath of God is real, but it is not the source of the kind of fear that draws us close to God, like we're scared to go anywhere else. It is not the thing that draws us closer out of panic or anxiety. The thing that gets us closer to God and is the essence of the "fear of the Lord" is humility.

The fear of the Lord is about dealing humbly within God's authority like we deal with things like gravity. It calls us into respect of life as we find it, of ourselves, of others, and into learning the nature of the one in charge. Wisdom teaches us how the world and we work.

Fearing God is a call to humility, to admitting we do not know everything. Being humble before God is the beginning of wisdom. It is learning to utilize the full measure of God's instructions and to let someone who knows how the path works make the path work for us.

Chapter Seven

But Isn't God Mad at Us Sinners?

I USED TO THINK that God was angry. Not always, but I read the Old Testament, and I knew the stories. God's wrath is one of the main things that causes people to hesitate about, argue against, and even use as a reason to walk away from God. But what if God is not mad at us but mad at what separates us from him? What if God hates the stress, trauma, disconnection and damage we live in everyday, even more than we do? I used to think God was mad at people, but I learned that God's anger is directed at the environment we create when we walk away from loving God and loving others.

BEST WORDS

As we consider the examples of God's wrath that we find in the Bible we need to remember that we are reading the best words people had to describe the experience they were having. In the book of Revelation, John tells us that the streets of heaven are paved with gold and that there is a sea of glass like crystal. I have to admit that when I get to heaven, if the streets are not actually paved with gold, I am not going to complain. My point is that John described to us an overwhelming experience and the Holy Spirit inspired John's *best words* from that experience to do that. I get the picture from what he wrote, and it sounds (and I expect it will be) amazing, truly indescribable, so I have no need to hold him to it exactly as the final experience of heaven. The inspiration of the Holy Spirit doesn't require John to tell us exactly how things will be anymore than our Bibles need to only be read in Hebrew and Greek. God has given us a freedom in our expression that allows us to say God's truth in a way that we can understand.

People have suggested that every word in the original manuscripts was exactly as God wanted them. They use that to say that the original manuscripts were *inerrant*—without flaw or mistake. The trouble with this is that it holds us to a standard we can never find. We can never find the original manuscripts, but people continue to suggest and act like they are accessible even though we carry translations and interpretations around with us. This attitude encourages and supports our seeking a level of purity that is only an idol. God didn't demand that his Word never be translated. He sent it out to be expressed as clearly and plainly as it could be to every person on the planet. The truth that is most important in the Bible is understood by anyone who reads it. The other stuff, the things we argue over or make our favorite aspects or approaches, is just a conversation. We get to talk about the ideas of Scripture, to dig in to find, as best we can, the experience of the people who first had the experience, who first wrote it out, who first heard it. God isn't worried about those things. The stuff that's most important to understand, anyone can understand.

The real problem with trying to hang onto inerrancy is that God does not seem to care as much as we do if we get the words of the book exact. When I realized that God was not a controlling God and then saw that he did not feel a need to control the Bible, my perspective shifted. I have learned never to use the word *inerrant* but to use the word *true*. I believe the Bible is true, and the fact that it is true is what gives the Bible its authority. The purpose of the Bible is to help us open up a living and daily conversation with the ever-present God. God doesn't speak only through the pages of the Bible but intimately and deeply within people's souls.

God has allowed the original manuscripts to disappear. God has allowed our later copies to be translated into almost every language in the world. That requires approximation of ideas, colloquialism in phrases, and even the shifting of allusions to fit into a cultural context. There are religions that demand that their holy book be read only in one language, or that God's truth can only be handled by one person. Christianity does not do that and has continually walked away from that. Quite plainly, God is not as worried about controlling the exact words as much as having people grow in relationship with him. God gave us the Holy Spirit as our constant companion, to walk us into the truth of Jesus daily, as we live. It is not a stretch to suggest that God's more concerned with authenticity in life and the experience of truth in authenticity that is lived vividly and relationally. God's truth is seen in how the world actually works and how we live with each other.

So, as we talk about the wrath of God, it might be good to begin by recognizing that God has a "long nose." In Hebrew, the word for "anger" is also the same word for "nose." When it says that "God's anger burned against Israel," it is appropriate to have the image of nostrils flaring and one's nose getting red. As God says in Exod 34:6 that "I am big of nose," God is explaining that it takes a big deal and some time to get God's nose red and flaring. These are some of the Bible's best words for the experience of the anger of God.

They tell us that God is not full of vengeance or displeasure. We are told over and over that God is full of mercy, patience, and love. At the same time, we are told that the consequences of choosing separation from God will come down on us. Think again about the story of the sons and the father that Jesus told (Luke 15). The oldest son slaves away on the property, doing whatever he was told. Imagine his experience, going out to work each day, organizing the workers, explaining how the tools work, the fields respond, the ability to harvest and store away the crop, but always living under the burden of never making a mistake. His father would have taught him how to handle the work of the day, the months, the seasons. He took that all as law, as requirement, as necessary to gain approval of the father. He slaved.

The younger son was convinced he was as good as an orphan and that, essentially, his father was as good as dead. Imagine his growing up and watching the work of the older brother. Imagine his brother scolding him for trying something new or different, telling him over and over how to handle a tool, when to move, how to respond. He keeps giving orders and explaining that *this* is the way the father wants it done. Finally, the younger son has learned the "nature of the father" through the words and example of the older brother. He has no relationship with the father because what he's learned of life has been filtered through the words of the slavish son. "Give me my inheritance, now," he says to this one whom he now believes only wants another worker in the fields, and then goes off and wastes everything he's been given. As he leaves, he has broken rule after rule that the older son had tried to live by, down to simply disrespecting the father and demanding a gift of inheritance, that the father wasn't required to give.

The entire time the younger son is separated from his father, the father is watching for him, aching for him to return. He hates the distance between him and his son, he hates where his son is, he hates what his son is involved in, and he hates how his son can't see or hear his love. He hates the whole environment that surrounds his son. But he loves his son. The wrath of the father is not toward the son. It is toward what separates his son from him. If the son was to remain there, the wrath of his father would "remain with" him. That is, the wrath is "with" him and not "on" him. In John 3, toward the end of the chapter, we read a story of John the Baptist proclaiming the truth about Jesus, and John becomes quite deeply theological at the end of his speech. In that moment, he says, "Whoever believes in the Son has eternal life, but whoever rejects the Son will not see life, for God's wrath remains on them" (v. 36). We translate the word as "on," but it, again, can also mean "with." Why don't we translate it that way?

The older son won't come into the party celebrating the new life of his returned brother, whom he refers to as "this son of yours" when the father comes out to him as well. This older son believed he was a slave and says, "I have slaved for you for years," and that his father was the taskmaster. Again, the father won't abide that separation but seeks to reorient this son's understanding. "Everything belongs to you" is the literal truth. In Jewish law the older son owned everything. The father gave away a portion of the estate, but everything that was left now belonged to the elder son.

This is true of us as well, either of these depictions. We can so easily miss the reality of life with God. We do not live as if we have the full resources of God and life at hand. The wrath of God is against this kind of separation as well.

When someone lives choosing to separate themselves from God, they will not see the full potential of life, not the life that God deeply desires each of us and all of us to live. The wrath of God, that fierce anger, is the atmosphere in which this person lives, because it is filled with every element of destructive counterpart to grace, to love, to relationship. This person is still loved by God, but the powers, the influences, the consequences, even our choices that grow out of their misunderstandings or desperation to control life are all things that rip God's heart because they pull the person away. God hates the circumstance in which we find ourselves when we have cut off connection from him. But God loves us. Nothing can separate us from the love of God in Christ.

WHAT ABOUT SIN, AND DOESN'T GOD HATE SINNERS?

If we take it that God is into commandments and, thereby, really focused on us keeping the rules, then sin is breaking the rules, and God hates us for doing that. We are saying that God is not interested in healing but in ruling. But, if God is working to heal the world, then, like with a physician, the biggest worry is not how or why the damage happened. The biggest issue is getting the damage healed. God's healing works into the why and the how of the damage, drawing us away from it and toward our continuing to live in a way that supports healing. God is not focused on the breaking of rules because sin is not about rules. Sin is about death.

People of all different types, Christian and non-Christian, atheist and agnostic, believer and the almost uninterested, have asked me about sin. "You Christians say 'we sin,' that 'we are sinners.' What exactly is sin?" There are a couple of really important answers to this question, but they both have to do with death, the deadening of responsiveness and the deadening of communication. To get to those answers, whoever the person has been who asked about sin, I asked them this question. "If you could cheat on the person who loves you best, and they would never know, they would never find out, would something inside you still die?" Everyone, from any background or lifestyle, I've asked has said, "Yes." I believe that is because we all know it is true.

"That," I tell them, "that bit of death . . . that is sin."

Sin has a spiritual impact on us. It damages us as spiritual beings. When we sin, we kill off part of the thing that makes a relationship work, whether it is with another person, with God, or with the created world. (We all know we can do lasting damage to nature and the world, and when we do, something inside us dies. After that, we're able to do more in the same manner.) Sin is the deadening that happens within our soul of something that should work. Some part that should be responsive, reliable, regularly engaged stops functioning as it should. The more we repeat that same choice, the more death pervades our soul.

I went to a gym and hired a trainer to help me get in shape. In my initial physical assessment, I was asked to do as many push-ups as I could. I went down on the ground and found I could not push myself off the floor, not an inch. I have always been able to do at least twenty push-ups, so I was dumbfounded. The trainer did some more testing and then sent me to my doctor and, there, we discovered that one shoulder was not responsive. In an accident, some time before, I had dislocated my shoulder bones and stretched out the tendons in my shoulder. They were no longer working as they should. I chose not to get an operation at that time, so the trainer put me on a series of workouts that included rebuilding muscles around my shoulder to compensate.

Imagine how things within us spiritually can die and stop responding as they should as well. Muscles can atrophy when they're not used. Areas of our bodies can lose their liveliness just from a lack of use. We can do similar damage within our souls. Parts of us—emotional, moral sensitivities toward others or God, all parts of our soul—can die little by little as we choose to hurt someone or someone's feelings even, to come up with excuses rather than confessions, to lie instead of admitting and dealing with the truth, to stop participating in helping others' lives, to try to get our own way. That dying off, which can grow throughout our soul, is the sin that God hates. God hates death. It will be the enemy that dies last, we're told in the book of Revelation.

We have people in the world who are making the doing of damage to each other a stimulating experience, even sexual. For whatever reason, people are accepting being treated as unworthy, valueless, and becoming willing to be damaged. We have others who handle incarcerations who treat those who have been found guilty of some crime as inferior. There are people in the world whose level of responsibility produces a growing expectation of control; it's a demand that people respond to their position and authority. When someone doesn't accept that authority or rebels against it, there are people who respond not with strength but with panicked wrath. What can be truly frightening is that people of faith can do this thinking they are imitating or even acting on the behalf of God. All of this reveals a level of death within the soul of the person. The individual who commits a crime is, sometimes, just acting out from the death that's been growing inside them for years.

Sin is death because what should be responsive to God's communication with us gets cut off. Picture two mountain climbers on a high mountain, tied to each other. They need the rope because one can become the anchor if the other slips and falls. One can become the guide if they can't see each other because they're lost in a fog. In a similar way, imagine that there was a rope that tied every person in the world to every other person in the world. Sin is when I try to kill that connection. Sin is when I pull out my "knife of self-centeredness," or anger, or personal preference or superiority, and cut a strand of the rope that ties me to someone else. We connect still, just that much less. We do not feel them as much. We do not recognize how close we are as much. We act like we do not need them in the world as much. I am pretending that we are not interdependent as humanity. The more I cut into the connection, the less I feel, the deader I become and the more separated I am.

At the time of this writing, there is a pandemic sweeping the world. We have been taught in the most serious of terms how interdependent we are. The entire population of the world has seen that we can easily kill those around us just by breathing on them. We can lose the ones we love best by being careless of how we care for them or by our protection of them. We have had the reality of interdependence beaten into us daily. This wasn't taught to us, however, as a lesson but shown to us as a revealed truth. It doesn't make a difference how we respond to the illness, whether we believe in it and the vaccinations we are offered or not. We may cut ahead of people to get our vaccine first, or we may deny the contagious nature of the illness by our actions, but the truth of our interconnectedness has been displayed for months. If you reject the nature or danger of the illness, just think about the supply-chain problems, the financial impact on villages, towns, and cities. When we cut the ties we have with others, we kill a piece of ourselves that should work.

With God, our connection is more like a fiber-optic cable where hundreds of lines of communication are connecting us with the Spirit. Every time I reach up and cut into that line, I destroy the flow of information between myself and God. When I do not want to hear God, do not want to pay attention, do not like the way I am feeling, and so cut through the line that is bringing me God's questions or his heart's guidance, I just slice away a bit more. And as I do, I tell God, "You're as good as dead to me," or "do not bother me," or "I'm busy doing all the rules you set up for me. I have the information you sent. You gave me the rules. I do not need to spend time with you. I have to get my job done for you." The lines of communication go dead little by little.

When I was a little guy, about three years old, my mom was ironing something on our kitchen counter. We had one of those pass-throughs from the kitchen, that is, a counter with stools. My mom finished her ironing and picked up the big thing she was working on to carry it into another room, but then she stopped. She looked at me and said, "Now, do not touch the iron. It is hot."

And what do you think I did as soon as she was out of the room?

I clambered up one of the stools and put my hand right on the iron. My mom came rushing back as she heard me cry out. I was already down on the floor again as she asked if I touched the iron. Now, what do you think she wanted most in that moment?

Do you think her main thought was to punish me? No! She wanted to know the truth so she could heal me. Jesus came to teach us that God is like a loving mom who wants to heal the world.

SO, HELL CAN BE REAL

At that moment I had a choice, just like I had a choice not to follow my mom's guidance. I could have stuck my hand in my pocket and not shown it to her. I could have kept my hand in my pocket, even though it was killing me. And it would have been killing me, more than just the pain, but spiritually and relationally. It would have been deadening a part of my soul, the relational connection and the lines of communication I had with my mom. If I had kept my hand in my pocket and refused her care, I would allow that deadening to grow. If the damage was bad enough and got infected, it could grow until it killed me. Instead of admitting the truth, of agreeing with her that I needed healing, I would be separating myself from her.

The deadening within us is sin. This is the consequence of breaking relationship. Whether it is relating with God, relating with another person or a people, group, race, gender, religion, or some aspect of the created world that depends on our participation in its worth—whatever—sin is the deadening of a piece of our soul. Some part of us stops working as it should. The more we make the choice to separate, the deeper and wider death grows in our souls.

This is the doorway to hell, as Jesus describes it.

When Jesus describes hell, it is always in terms of separation between persons and the deep regret experienced by the one who judges, or dismisses the worth of, or separates herself or himself from others. When Jesus describes judgment, he tells us that we judge ourselves. Our judgment of others is death in our souls. It is our own words and actions, but it is even our casual comments that reveal our ingrained attitudes, he says (Matt 12:36–37). Our separation is revealed by how we live towards others. This is what will judge us. When Jesus describes judgment, he tells us that it is revealed from within each person and the consequences are described as the deepest experience of regret.

We will know what we could have done, how we could have lived, for whom and in how many ways we could have expressed care, unity, life-giving support, and how, instead, we watched out for and took care of ourselves. And when that is revealed, we are overcome by darkness, the burning, worm-eating-from-within, gnashing-of-teeth experience that will be hell. Jesus told us that hell will be something we choose and not something into which God tosses us. We will have chosen to reject God entirely. The thing is that hell may not be for eternity.

But if, as that tiny guy who touched the iron, I had jammed my hand in my pocket, not allowing the healing by my mom, the deadening of my soul could have produced further rebellion and rejection, eventually toward my mom and her hopes and desires for me. I could have practiced separation until I was breaking her heart, doing personal damage to her or to myself and our family, and finally either leaving or destroying my home. This is the story of so many people in the world.

And, if, at the end of all things, I suddenly was touched but unconvinced by and deadened to the reality of God's loving heart that I had rejected, I would continue to choose leaving, rather than returning. The darkness that would surround me at that time would be of my own making. Jesus explains to us that hell is of our own making. We can end with hearts that never want anything to do with God, but is there a way out of hell?

Theologians and storytellers have speculated on whether God will give us another chance in that moment. There have been numerous suggestions on how God could still make a difference, still call us back after this life. The description by Jesus does not challenge any of those possibilities. Still, the point of Jesus' coming was to call us back to God now. The point of Jesus' coming was to demonstrate what life looks like, what a human being looks like when they are never disconnected from God. Jesus came to give us more than eternal life. He came to create a new society in which we can live now. When we turn toward this, we walk out of the darkness of not recognizing the worth of others and how we diminish their worth.

I was teaching a Sunday school program for high schoolers that included a host of juniors and seniors (people who do not normally show up for Sunday school). A young man, who was a regular part of things, was not in class that day. About halfway through the time, I saw him pass by the window in the door of the room. He was looking in. Some little time later, I caught him going by again, looking in, making sure we made eye contact.

A third time, he came by, not long before the class ended, and this time he stopped, making sure that I saw him and that we were looking at each other.

After class, I found him down the hall in an empty classroom and we stood and talked. It struck me that he looked dirty. Not only were his clothes dark, but they looked used, worn and his hair was greasy, unkempt. He just did not seem washed. I asked him what was going on, and he began to explain his story of the night before. He attended a private school and a classmate, a girl, and he were studying together in his dorm room. And it got late. As they were finishing, they speculated on spending the night together. Without emotional attachment, without an interest in creating a relationship, with no real connection other than their age, their proximity, and the opportunity, they had intercourse.

He woke up feeling like something was lost within him. He did not like how he had made use of this friend. That morning, he knew it was his regular time to come to church, to come to class and to see me, but he couldn't get there. He still wanted to see me, though, so, he came late after sending the young woman off into her day. He felt dirty within, he said, and I shared my observation on how it was revealed on his outsides as well. He agreed, disheartened. We talked over what happened and how it made him feel. He was filled with regret toward himself, toward the girl, toward God. We talked about the death he had created in his soul and what could be done about that. We prayed for God's help in that moment.

He left me intending to find the girl and to say, for his part, he was sorry and that she meant more to him as a person than he had shown through his actions. He wanted her to know that he didn't want to just use her. Some time later, he listened to and reconsidered the story of the work of Jesus on the cross, his death and his rising again into life. He came by one evening, overwhelmed with joy, feeling whole and new. It was in discovering the truth and the ability to communicate with God that his heart leapt free. He could not stop expressing this as we talked, laughingly describing how everything seemed suddenly special, particular, and clearer. It was like he was seeing it all, he said, seeing everything for the first time.

"It is like you've been born again," I said.

"Yes!" he said, buoyantly, but then he stopped, his face clouding, and his hand coming up between us, as he said, "Whoa! Whoa!"

He had grown up in an atmosphere that rejected "born again" as a label, as a political position and as an agenda. I pointed out that Jesus did not use it as a label or politically, but as an experience. I said, "You are experiencing what Jesus talked about. You do not need to use the label to describe yourself. It was only one of the ways Jesus described this truth. You just need to know the truth of the reality and live into it." And he did.

The core of the Christian message is that Jesus took all the death produced within our souls, by all the choices we make toward separation, onto himself. He became death (sin) so that we might know life. And not only life, but the justice of God. We're told that Jesus became sin so that we could become the righteousness of God. That word "righteousness" is also our word "justice." It is translated that way in different places. What would it mean if we became the "justice" of God? What if it meant that we tasted God's justice that was seeking to show us our worth all along? It's a "justness," a "rightness," that should be experienced by every person. Suppose Jesus' death brought about justice, as God understands justice, as *this* is the way things should be in the life of this person. This is what they should be experiencing.

If you know the story of *Les Misérables*, and the moment where Jean Valjean is hauled back by the police to the priest, from whom he has stolen silverware, you know he is waiting to be condemned. The priest, to everyone's astonishment, agrees that he gave the silverware to Valjean and gives him even more silver. Justice from the priest is experienced as truly just. And like that, justice from God looks like mercy and grace. This is a judge who understands our predicament, our struggles, and provides us with justice that speaks into our reality, our true circumstance, and not just into breaking a rule or law. Jean Valjean has the darkness of his soul cleaned out in that moment. He moves into a new life.

The change within us that comes from realizing that we can give up, clear up, and be healed from the death within us is the new life Jesus promised. It is the new life found within that changes the way we live as what should have been working within us begins working again. It comes back to life again. We come back into communication with God again, and then we can become the *justice* or *just-ness* that other people need in their own lives. Then our good news, our Gospel, becomes truly good and truly news. It comes as an unexpectedly just way of treating others that surprises and challenges the way the world runs without God.

This is why people (and Jesus himself) describe it as being "born again." God's greatest desire is for us to come to him, to find a new recreated life, and to live within the instructions that reveal the inner workings of the world and relationships, that cause life to flourish and that lead us to love God, to love other people, and to love the world, truly and deeply. But, what about the one who never gets the chance?

There are people who essentially live their lives on a four-to-eight-block layout in any city. They almost never go farther than four blocks in any direction and only know what is offered of life within that distance. Suppose that a young man in that setting grows up there seeking to find anything that will present more than a life that is based on survival. But it seems like he doesn't have any choice. He must survive. He steals food, he steals stuff, he steals money, gradually gathering or finding around himself a community of like-minded young people taking advantage of any weakness they can find in the system or in an individual to make it through the day. Suppose his heart grows hard, deadened by using others, hurting others, dismissing connections with anyone other than those who are making similar choices.

This young man makes use of anything that proves he belongs to his group, which includes the gang rape of a nine-year-old girl who went just a little too far into the wrong neighborhood. He and his buddies teach her, and anyone connected to her, a severe lesson. In retaliation, the people who know that little girl shoot and kill one of his friends. He hops in a carload of friends, intent on delivering an even clearer message that no one messes with them in any way. The drive-by shooting does not go cleanly. Someone in the other neighborhood is fast enough to open up on the car and he gets hit with a bullet that ends his life.

As he opens his eyes on the other side of eternity, looking into the face of God, hearing the reality of God's heart for the first time, what if everything he had never known is suddenly presented to him. What if, in that moment, he says from the fullness of his soul: "You're what I've always wanted."

Do you think God, in that moment, will say "too bad"? Or do you think it is possible God will say, "I know . . ."? Would God be able to wash away his regret in that moment? Would God know the full experience of this person and be able to present his love to him for the first time? We must take judgment out of our hands and leave it to God.

Where does your hope lie when it comes to the judgment of others? Does it lie in your own ability to decide who is in and who is out? Or does it lie in God's hands, in God's wisdom, and in God's ability to know each heart? Jesus said to leave judgment up to God and, instead, to give ourselves over to the work of loving others into significance.

HOW THE BIBLE LOOKS AT A HOPELESS CASE

In the Bible there is the story of a king named Manasseh. He ruled the southern part of the region we refer to as Israel called the kingdom of Judah. The northern part of the country continued to be called Israel, but by the time of Manasseh it was overrun by invaders and no longer existed as it was. Manasseh, it says, "did evil in the eyes of the Lord." He did evil in the eyes of people as well.

We know of Manasseh outside of the Bible's account of him.[1] This ruler tried to wipe out the worship of God, setting up idols and creating practices that were like the people around Israel. He had no relationship with God and in some ways seemed to hate his own people. In one description, not found as graphically in the Bible, we read that Manasseh killed so many of his own people in Jerusalem that the streets became muddy from the blood.

One interesting thing about the story of Manasseh is that it is told twice. We find it in the book of 2 Kings and in the book of 2 Chronicles. In the first telling, we learn that Manasseh was as bad as bad could be and then he dies. The one account ends there. But, in the second, his debauchery is presented plainly, until it says that the king of Babylon marches in, captures Manasseh, puts a hook through his nose, ties the hook to the back of a horse and leads Manasseh out of the country that way. He is humiliated before all his people. When he is imprisoned in Babylon, Manasseh, we read in 2 Chronicles, turns to God, admits his regret, and agrees with God's views. He is given the chance to return to Judah, gets back and turns his life around. He leads the people back into relationship with God.

It appears that, for some people, the story of Manasseh is summed up in his dying after being a cruel tyrant. For others, Manasseh's full story is not finished until we get to enjoy his change after his regret is washed away.

God is not mad at us. He is furious at the circumstances that separate us from him. He is always ready to bring healing to our lives and to lead us back into living. The best news for us, when we want to be the judge, is that this is for anyone, everyone, even the people we believe would never listen or never care.

Is there a political leader, a political party, a boss, an employee, a neighbor or even a relative, whose story you want to see ended with their death? Or do you want to leave yourself open to God's love being stronger than your judgment? Who will God condemn? Jesus says we do not want to

---

1. Josephus, *Complete Works*, 10.3.1

be involved in that. In fact, he says, we can't do it. He said, "Do not condemn or you will be condemned," which is the natural result. Our condemnation grows from the death within us that came from us separating ourselves from those whom we condemn. This is why we are told to love our enemies.

How hard is that?!

Chapter Eight

Where Everything Is in Place

LOVING OUR ENEMIES, PEOPLE who desire the worst for us, is one of the most difficult experiences. Normally, even naturally, we are looking for revenge on enemies and not for their well-being. And that expresses the core of our separation from God. We are brought face to face with this in Matt 5:43–45:

> You have heard that it was said, 'Love your neighbor and hate your enemy.' But I tell you, love your enemies and pray for those who persecute you, that you may be children of your Father in heaven. He causes his sun to rise on the evil and the good, and sends rain on the righteous and the unrighteous.

We have a perspective on people, good, bad, or indifferent. God has a heart for all people because God actually knows what leads people into their manner of living. He knows the generational impact of abuse and neglect wherever its source, from society's acts of injustice or hatred or parental damage. God knows everything from the dysfunction of our brain, to the abuse we've suffered, to the misinterpretation someone has toward something done or said that turns people against each other. And God is completely present in the life of each person on the planet, working to change the outcome.

This is different from the picture some people paint of God as "all-loving." It appears, sometimes, when people describe what they mean by "all-loving" that God is also "not-seeing." It is as if we are being told that God is just completely encouraging, completely warm and happy and, also, complacent and docile. But God recognizes persecution, evil and unrighteousness and God hates it. Take it another way . . .

What if God is actually God and not an oversized human being? What if God knows exactly why we do what we do?

What if God actually knows when any sparrow falls in the world? That would mean that God knows every waterfall, every sunset, the growth of every blade of grass. It would also mean that God knows the spinning of every planet, the sound produced by a nebula, the celestial architecture that becomes a supernova. What if God knows . . .

What if God understands atomic theory? What if everything from molecules to microbes are actually within God's view every day, every moment? What if God knows not just what fires the mirror neurons in our brains but what they are accomplishing when they do? What if God knows exactly how red blood cells push their way through membranes and deliver all the life-giving goods to all the various parts of the body by doing that and why it is important that they do it that way?

Spiritually, the design of God is that all things work together for good for those who love him and are called according to his purpose. God will use all things whether useless, destructive, or gratuitous to work to the benefit of those who love him. The witness of the universe is that the overall design of God is making all things work together. From the Bible we learn that God gets why they don't when they don't, but we also learn that God's design is to bring all things into wholeness, where each part connects and supports each other part. The design of God is that all things work together.

What if God does know exactly why we do what we do?

What if God knows why we can't kick our habits, even why we can't even postpone our habits? What if God knows why there is breakdown between friends, lovers, neighbors, or countries? What if God knows what makes us walk past the needs of others, or avoid seeing the headlines, or skim over the news feed? What if God knows what's happening to the contours of our brains as we binge watch through the fifth episode in one evening? What if God knows that we have an ache within us that is not just produced by our nucleotides but by something even more fundamental to our being, something deeper than our DNA? What if God knows, and what if what God desires most is that our core structural makeup align with him, get justified with his design to make all things work together?

What if God knows exactly why we do what we do? And what if God doesn't hate us for it? What if God loves us even though God knows it all?

What if God knows why we do everything from breaking others' hearts to genocide? What if God knows that it all stems from a piece of ourselves that died? This piece of ourselves that we broke when we lied to the person who loves us best, when we cheated, when we chose something shallow instead of deep and enduring. What if it broke because of what was done to us, something over which we had no control, but it damaged us so deeply that we can't believe there is a God who cares about us? Or what if instead of truly participating in God's design of the created nature of the world, relationships with others, or relationship with God, we damaged ourselves, our planet, and others, because of our wants, our need for control, or because of the hurt we live in, we just began lashing out and destroying whatever we could?

Our ache to fulfill our want, our control, our ache grows into what separates us from God's design and from God. So, why isn't God doing something about it? We want magic so badly. We want God to change all these terrible things, to stop them from ever starting, to make it all perfect. We don't really want to God to heal us in genuine ways, ways that take time, that require growth and maturing. We ache for a quick fix, to just make the frustration stop, while God is looking for us to become fully functioning human beings. What we don't seem to see is that God wants us . . . as us. He wants us to be partners with him in making the world work, but he wants us as thinking partners, as beings who are engaged with knowing, understanding, and participating in the world with him. The trouble is that he has to clear up the damage within our souls in order to communicate with us clearly, so we will begin to choose the things that he would choose.

We're told that God's answer to that ache in our souls is Jesus, who came to teach us that God so loved the world, each of us and all of this, to provide us with an example of what a human being looks like when they are constantly connected with God. Jesus gave up the ability to control in order that he might demonstrate to us what kind of strength we have outside of trying to control life. He came with the power to destroy death, to heal us, and then to bring us back into God's design. We're told that whoever believes in him, that is, follows him, will heal that separation from how he designed us to be and see it restored. Jesus' life, teaching, death, and resurrection reveals how God accomplished that in the realest of ways, in our ways, through a real life, so we could recognize that we are loved more than we can imagine, and we could find a pathway into living truly and fully.

I believe all this means that God is not "not-seeing" when we say God is all-loving. I believe it means that God is all loving in the sense of all-knowing and all-understanding and completely engaged with the reality of how our world, existence, and true healing works. God knows why and how everything happens. Our excuses and our attempts at purity with our provisos of "good enough" do not fool God or make God wink, because God knows that reality lies even deeper. God knows what we are doing to the interior nature of our souls and how it separates us from him or from others. God knows, and it breaks God's heart. So, we find that God is at work in bringing it back together, bringing it into harmony with himself and his heart. Jesus' role, at least in part, is to demonstrate how God desires us to act. Jesus is not only bringing creation back to God but showing us what a life looks like when it is in partnership with God. Jesus does not excuse us or teach us that God doesn't care that much about poor or even devastating choices we make. Instead, Jesus shows us that God sees it, knows it, and is working against it to bring us true healing.

IF GOD KNOWS, ISN'T GOD TO BLAME?

When we lay out the picture of God being all-knowing, and we consider that God is seeking to shape the world to end up where he wants it to end up, then isn't he responsible for my father's horrible death from cancer, for my dog getting hit by that car that never even slowed down, for the breakdown in communication with my nephew? Isn't God responsible for it all?

If God is not seeking control, then he is not seeking even the little bit of control that we might suggest is within "being in charge." We would like that because then there would be a target for our frustration, our venting, our pain and, intriguingly, God seems willing to receive that even if it paints him in a bad light. God doesn't seem to be worried over our taking aim at him. Read Ps 13:

> How long, Lord? Will you forget me forever?
> How long will you hide your face from me?
> How long must I wrestle with my thoughts
> and day after day have sorrow in my heart?
> How long will my enemy triumph over me?
> Look on me and answer, Lord my God.
> Give light to my eyes, or I will sleep in death,
> and my enemy will say, "I have overcome him,"

and my foes will rejoice when I fall.
But I trust in your unfailing love;
my heart rejoices in your salvation.
I will sing the Lord's praise,
for he has been good to me.

To me, this sounds like someone standing out in a field under the sky and shaking their fist as they scream upward. This is only one of the psalms that seems to make God the target of our venting. God allowed that to be part of our Bibles. God seems to be okay with taking the brunt of our lack of understanding and anger and pain. It seems to me that God wants us to do that. I believe he wants us to do that because he is the one who isn't hurt by it. He knows the reasons for it, but he also knows the benefit to us, within our souls when we vent. He also knows the limits to our understanding and the frustrations those cause. We need to remember Jesus, kneeling in the garden of Gethsemane, praying alone, and aching in the experience of his own limitations. We need to remember this so that we also recall something of what he gave up in joining us in a human existence.

It benefits us to scream out our anger and weep out our frustrations to God. As we do that, however, we are coaxed by this psalm, if not regularly by God's Spirit, to also recognize that there is more to life, and something more trustworthy in God, than my despair. That word "but" in verse 5 is a shift point. It leads into an expectation that God will demonstrate his love and kindness because that's his character. It expresses that we know that we don't understand everything. We know we have limitations, and so we're encouraged by them to continue to trust that God is going to come through, although we may not be able to see how at this moment. We may, just now, want to blame him for it all, and it appears that he is okay with that.

But God is not who is responsible for this stuff going wrong.

If we have created a toxic environment within our bodies, by the products we choose to make and use . . . then it's not God who is responsible. He gives us the wisdom to deal with them. We are responsible, and we have learned, there are companies we work for and work with that are responsible. In this world of interdependence, we have the call and need to care for every other person and if we move profit into a higher priority than care for others, we deaden something within our souls that is supposed to be working. This is why the love of money is the root of tremendous evil.

We are both given and called into wisdom to know the world that has been created for us, of which we are to be a part and not owners.

We need to find out how the world works. When we discover that one aspect of a plant makes us sick, like tomato leaves, while another part of the same plant is healthy and life-giving, like tomatoes, then we can realize that life is more a matter of us finding out how life actually works and participating in that than about us demanding that God wield control over everything.

God is not a genie granting wishes, any more than God is just a bigger human being with superpowers seeking minute control over every aspect of life. God is loving and will walk with us through all the kinds of things Jesus also walked through. God understands our circumstance and calls us to find the wisdom that he is, to discover the way he and the world works, and how they work together. We are called to be partners with God.

We discover this as we study the words of Jesus, words that call us into deeper wisdom, words that help us to see a God who knows, understands, and loves us. Words that may be said with a different tone of voice than we've experienced before.

Chapter Nine

The Deeper Wisdom

WE NEED TO LOOK closely at Jesus' words and think on them as the tone of voice of God. When we enter Jesus' words, we walk into the atmosphere of God's grace, because this was the person who was the most attentive to God's voice. In fact, Jesus was God's voice. From the end of the first century after his birth, his followers have called him "the Word." One of the best places to start is with the fullest statement of Jesus' teaching, the Sermon on the Mount.

In Matthew 5:3–10, he said:

> "Blessed are the poor in spirit,
> for theirs is the kingdom of heaven.
> Blessed are those who mourn,
> for they will be comforted.
> Blessed are the meek,
> for they will inherit the earth.
> Blessed are those who hunger and thirst for righteousness,
> for they will be filled.
> Blessed are the merciful,
> for they will be shown mercy.
> Blessed are the pure in heart,
> for they will see God.
> Blessed are the peacemakers,
> for they will be called children of God.
> Blessed are those who are persecuted because of righteousness,
> for theirs is the kingdom of heaven."

The Beatitudes or blessings with which Jesus begins the Sermon on the Mount are statements that may have seriously confused and, yet, sparked hope in those listening when he first said them. It would be sort of like, "I'm not sure I'm getting what he's saying, because it sounds different from what we've been taught. But if he's saying what I think he's saying then I like it." If we start with the understanding that humility is the fear of the Lord, and the fear of the Lord is the beginning of wisdom, then humility is the beginning of wisdom; then we begin by seeking to be attentive to the words of Jesus. The Beatitudes is where Jesus starts.

In one way, he begins by speaking to people who feel separated from God. If we did not practice the initial instructions given to the people at the base of Mount Sinai, we might feel like the first part of each of his initial blessings, was about us and that could feel very confusing. People listening might be identifying with the ideas of being "poor in spirit," "mourning," or "meek" spiritually. The first three instructions of Sinai told us—actually, told the ancestors of the people listening to Jesus as he spoke—that we are not to put any other power into God's face, not to seek control through our own efforts and not to seek control through misusing our relationship with God. So, Jesus' initial teaching here speaks into the hearts of people who would know that they have not lived that way but have lived against God. They have lived seeking to do it on their own, sometimes because it feels like it's the only way for them to survive and other times because it's just the best they can do with what they have. Jesus says to them and us, "if you realize that you have lived separated from God, using whatever power or powers you can lay your hands on or can create for yourself, and you don't know how to do it any other way, but you want it to be another way, then cheer up. You're blessed. You're well off. You're already standing in the kingdom of heaven." This is being "poor in spirit."

He says that if we know we have nothing to offer God, nothing that works well spiritually, that we don't have the nice, god-focused, churchy answers within us, that we are "poor" in spirit, we should feel happy (blessed). If we come before God mournful, sad, and sorry for all we've lost or for what could have been in our lives, we should feel blessed or well-off. If we come before God with subdued spirits, ones that have been disciplined into willingness to receive whatever directions God might want to give, that is "meeked," that we should feel fortunate. We're well off.

Jesus' first disciples were men who might know, casually but clearly, that they do not fit into the lifestyle of the Pharisees, scribes, priests, or

Levites, meaning people (some of them) who confidently approached God in the temple in Jerusalem and knew within themselves that they were the ones God loved. The disciples are the people who gather up around Jesus wondering, even a bit bewilderedly, that he wants them as his students. Rabbis usually picked the ones they thought were the best. They might be wondering if this is for real. Who was in and who was out of God's good grace was clear to anyone in the country at that time. If you kept the rules, kept the right company, or if you were rich and well-connected, you were in. God obviously loved you. The men and women around Jesus initially knew that trying to keep up with the requirements of "purity" would have always been a challenge, if not out of reach realistically. "Doing the best we can" could have almost been a mantra, but their perspective would more likely have been one of giving up any inner assurance that they had any possibility of being as "good" as they *should be*. Others were easily better than they were.

Jesus calls them out of competition and out of judging themselves and others, out of the struggle for purity and into a new insight into the true tone of voice of God. He begins by saying to those around him that if they feel that they don't actually measure up, then congratulations are in order. You are in just the right spot because you are already walking in the kingdom of God, you will find comfort and you will be given strength to live life fully. Humility, fearing the Lord, is just the best starting point because God can now work with you and lead you into life-giving instructions and guidance. If we don't have all the answers, God has the ability to get through to us and teach us his love, his insight, and his partnership.

"Inheriting" was a major source of strength in life in that culture. "Inheriting the earth" was then a statement saying that they would gain sufficient strength to live well in the world. This might be a difficult concept to grasp, but Jesus goes on leading them deeper. Imagine people getting excited as they begin to hear, and capture in their hearts, the spirit of what he is telling them about God. Even if they're not getting everything, his joy, his tone of voice is getting through.

If they hunger and thirst for righteousness, for the justness that everyone living and enjoying in this world should have, then they will find it. They will be filled, sated. In fact, they will start to produce it. They will provide it to others. Remember that Jesus wasn't talking about the righteousness of the Pharisees. Righteousness for many of them was a rigid construct of rules for living in purity. Righteousness that reflects *justice* creates a different goal in our minds than the idea of purity. Righteousness is not the purity of God as much as the "rightness" or "justness" that is found in God and that should be given to all people. It is not a level of supposed "holiness." Although, in light of what you may have already read here, it is the kind of holiness that is special, lived into, and invites everyone to be part of. It is the experience of justice, *rightness*, that should be given to all people. Jesus is telling them that if they ache to see that rightness in the world and in themselves, they will get what they are seeking.

Can you see how the ache for justice, for rightness for all, moves into mercy? If their humility has moved them into God's kingdom, his life in their hearts, then it makes them compassionate to others. It moves them away from looking down on those who are struggling around them, or up toward those who they've been taught are purer than them. If they've given up judgment, then they will receive the same kind of compassion. This honoring of all people produces an assurance of equality and then builds a level of character in their souls and in their actions. If they have integrity, a pure heart, in that they are not wishy-washy, not sometimes feeling better than others, or looking out for themselves more than sharing justice, while at other times trying to be good, which then gets "balanced" by them cheating at the edges of life, then they will see where God is at work in the world. The eyes of their souls will be opened, and they will recognize God's presence in the world. This isn't the kind of relationship with the world that our regular practice of seeking after "purity" produces. Jesus is talking about being one thing (having integrity) within ourselves, in our souls. Those seeking purity are trying to live by an overwhelming number of rules.

Jesus is walking his disciples into the spiritual forming of their souls, the work of the Holy Spirit. If they partner with God, living with God's direction, in creating wholeness in others' lives, bringing the rightness of healing into the lives of others or into the world, they will be seen by other people as children of God, children who reflect the true nature of their parent. They will be creating peace, that is "wholeness" or *shalom*. And if they find themselves harassed or oppressed by some people because they are treating others justly, or are talking about God's grace in this way to those whom these people don't see as worthy, with a "rightness" that should be given to all human beings, then they will be walking in the kingdom of God. They'll be in partnership with God and living in God's guidance. It will become their environment even if they're persecuted for it. They'll be in the company of the prophets of the Old Testament, who were also expressing the passionate heart of God. They, too, were persecuted, misunderstood, hated, and abused . . . but loved by God.

Jesus is telling his disciples that they are going to create a movement that works in this direction and so if they are harmed in any way for being part of it, they should be slapping high-fives with each other. They will find deep satisfaction and joy ultimately, because this is the same way the prophets of God were treated:

> Blessed are you when people insult you, persecute you and falsely say all kinds of evil against you because of me. Rejoice and be glad, because great is your reward in heaven, for in the same way they persecuted the prophets who were before you. (Matt 5:11-12)

Jesus opens up this new way of experiencing and living life with God because his own life was built on knowing the true tone of the voice of God and the instructions of God. If we follow him, learn his way of living, learn the wisdom he brings and share that with the world, we will become those who preserve life (salt) and bring hope (light) into the world.

This was the call of God through the instructions given at Sinai. And this is what was lost in the contract created by Nehemiah and Ezra. The people who realized that God's words, the warnings, that came through God's prophets had come true—that they had walked into destruction as a community because they didn't learn God's guidance—turned his instructions into commandments that were never to be broken or we would face God's wrath. These people should have been salt and light to the world, but they lost their way. So, Jesus comes to their descendants and re-establishes the direction of life in God and in the world, and the ability to hear God clearly:

> You are the salt of the earth. But if the salt loses its saltiness, how can it be made salty again? It is no longer good for anything, except to be thrown out and trampled underfoot.
> You are the light of the world. A town built on a hill cannot be hidden. Neither do people light a lamp and put it under a bowl. Instead, they put it on its stand, and it gives light to everyone in the house. In the same way, let your light shine before others, that they may see your good deeds and glorify your Father in heaven. (Matt 5:13-16)

Jesus is not calling his disciples to do "good deeds" so that God will love them more. He is calling on them to live in the rightness, the justice, that everyone should experience. This comes through living wisely. As they do that, their acts will reveal God's true nature to those around them. *Glorifying* is celebrating the revealing of the true nature of someone. It is like seeing someone enter a room and saying "there she is in all her glory."

Having established a core understanding of how to live in the rightness of God, like in the first three instructions of Sinai, Jesus provides his disciples with a profound, spiritual sense of rest. *Rest* is this deep gift of God. With *rest,* God leads people out of slavery of every kind. Later, in Matt 11:28–30, Jesus promises that following him will provide this:

> Come to me, all you who are weary and burdened, and I will give you rest. Take my yoke upon you and learn from me, for I am gentle and humble in heart, and you will find rest for your souls. For my yoke is easy and my burden is light.

Jesus' manner of working or living in the world relaxes our souls, removes the anxiety and panic we might experience as we try to find security or control in other powers. He calls his disciples into that peace as God is glorified or revealed by the way they live and treat others.

He then begins to work his way through the instructions on how to live with others, but he comes with a new tone of voice from the way the people have heard this guidance before. He brings the voice of God:

> "Do not think that I have come to abolish the Law or the Prophets; I have not come to abolish them but to fulfill them. For truly I tell you, until heaven and earth disappear, not the smallest letter, not the least stroke of a pen, will by any means disappear from the Law until everything is accomplished. Therefore anyone who sets aside one of the least of these *directions* and teaches others accordingly will be called least in the kingdom of heaven, but whoever practices and teaches these *directions* will be called great in the kingdom of heaven. (Matt 5:17-19)

As in Hebrew, the word used and translated as "command" is also the word for "direction" or "instruction." Jesus knows that as the disciples hear the difference in how he is bringing forth the instructions of God, that people will automatically question whether Jesus actually believes in them. He is challenging what they have been told and have tried to live with for centuries. He knows they have never heard this tone of voice from God before, so he assures them that what he is saying establishes the Law or guidance of God and the words of the Prophets in the core of their meaning and intention. This tone of voice sets these words free so that they can abundantly supply their purpose. He is telling them that these words they know were not wrong. They were absolutely correct, but they were not heard clearly. He is teaching them the fullness of them and is releasing the power of what they can do in establishing God's kingdom.

These are the words that will bring the justice or rightness into the life of every person on the planet. These are the words that will bring a sense of rightness within their own souls because they will see how they fit in God's kingdom, and how they are partnering with God to bring healing to the world. And because all these people listening to him know that there are people who are the "real" good people—Pharisees, priests, and teachers of the Law in the temple—he tells them that the way they live out this rightness of God has to be completely different from those who are so sure of themselves. It must be completely different because the rule keepers aren't part of the kingdom of God. They are not the ones who are close in on the presence of God in the world:

> For I tell you that unless your righteousness surpasses that of the Pharisees and the teachers of the law, you will certainly not enter the kingdom of heaven. (Matt 5:20)

At this point, Jesus begins to unpack the later instructions that were given on Sinai, and he starts in the most practical of ways. These are the ones that speak to how we should live with and treat each other. Rightness, that righteousness or justice, that God desires to see lived out in the world is not about gaining purity by being "good" or getting "gooder." It is found in relationship, how people are treated, and how they are lifted up to become all they can become. He does this by speaking about the two core attitudes of our hearts, our attitudes toward anyone, especially those who irritate us, and those who are most intimate to us, the ones we should treat with utmost justice. He talks about murder and adultery.

Jesus clarifies the terms of "murder" to become dismissing the worth of another person. He tells them that this instruction is not about just taking a life but treating that life, any other life, as worthless. This is not about just getting mad. It is about rejecting reconciliation. If we get to the place where we tell them that they are a waste of space, we condemn ourselves.

This is so important in our society at this time. People condemn or "cancel" or claim that anyone who disagrees with them is evil, and someone with whom no dialogue can happen. They deny the worth of anyone outside of their group or side. No exchange of ideas, no engagement with people as people, no exploration into the full life of the other gets done. Because we have moved into an era of electronic communication, we can cut someone off almost without a hearing. We can berate and belittle them, threaten and harass them until they disappear, get fired, get driven out of community or simply squirrel away into oblivion. Our keyboards have become loaded pistols.

Jesus is explaining the impact of our choices and attitudes on our own souls. When we dismiss the value of another life, remove from them the rightness they deserve as humans like ourselves, we deaden something within our own souls. We sin, that is, we create death, a deadening of a part of our soul that should work. The impact of the death we call sin on our souls is very real, and increasingly real within us, more than to the one we dismissed. When we do this kind of damage in a relationship, we not only terminate them in our lives, but we also terminate a part of our hearts that should work:

> "You have heard that it was said to the people long ago, 'You shall not murder, and anyone who murders will be subject to judgment.' But I tell you that anyone who is angry with a brother or sister will be subject to judgment. Again, anyone who says to a brother or sister, 'Raca [literally-empty head], is answerable to the court. And anyone who says, 'You fool!' will be in danger of the fire of hell. (Matt 5:21-22)

So, Jesus says that we are to work toward reconciliation, whether we are the ones who are angry or someone else is angry at us. We are working with God toward healing the world, and so it does not matter if we are the ones dismissing someone or the ones being dismissed. This is the most important thing in the world, bringing wholeness to relationships. It is more important than showing up with a gift for God. It is more important than our time and energy in other areas of life. Relationships are more important than issues. The life we live in relationship with others impacts their and our relationship with God. We need to be the people who work on getting things right with and bringing rightness to others:

> "Therefore, if you are offering your gift at the altar and there remember that your brother or sister has something against you, leave your gift there in front of the altar. First go and be reconciled to them; then come and offer your gift.
> "Settle matters quickly with your adversary who is taking you to court. Do it while you are still together on the way, or your adversary may hand you over to the judge, and the judge may hand you over to the officer, and you may be thrown into prison. Truly I tell

you, you will not get out until you have paid the last penny. (Matt 5:23-26)

Jesus shifts into an even more personal relational issue—marriage and adultery. Following along the lines of the original instructions, he tells the people that they need to be watchful to avoid deadening their hearts. If they begin to view people as objects, they begin to see them as something to be used, as having no worth other than to fulfill a felt need. So, instead of that, cut out that attitude, even if it hurts, maybe even leaves you feeling like you will be hampered by its loss. End it. Do not choose this for your soul, but see and teach your soul to continually see the worth in each person.

Jesus teaches them to recognize the violence inherent in damaging relationships. He brings up the seriousness of divorce that God says is "like a person clothing themselves in violence" (Mal 2:16). The certificate of divorce was a piece of legislation given by Moses, a permit by which the rupturing of the oneness created by intercourse and time would bring the least damage to the woman. Jesus says that if that oneness has already been broken by the woman's adultery, then divorce brings the least damage to the husband. But, in any case, marriage should be entered into with the intention of becoming one being with each other.

We must be careful as we handle the words of Jesus here. We have lived in response to being told we are following commandments, and so we have worked to tie everything to rule keeping. Think of how people have interpreted Jesus' words, especially here, to become new rules.

He starts by talking about the inner working of lust in our souls. He tells his disciples and us the effect on our souls when we give into the want and desire to use others' bodies. We are not treating them with value. They're just useable. Jesus tells us that this has the same impact on our souls as dismissing the worth of others when we commit adultery. We devalue the one to whom we say we are committed as well as the one whom we use while still living in that commitment. If we recognize that Jesus isn't creating new rules but explaining how reality works, we begin to see the depth of God's understanding of our souls and the damage we can do to them.

In Mark 10 we read that Jesus was approached by Pharisees with the question "Is it lawful for a man to divorce his wife?" He asked them what Moses directed. (Important to consider that Moses didn't command but gave directions.) And they say that Moses allowed it with a certificate of divorce. In other words, Moses created a process. To which, Jesus tells them that this is because their hearts were hard that Moses gave this guidance because people, in becoming married, are supposed to become one with each other.

It was natural for this rule to become a conversation among the Pharisees who were desiring to follow God's rules. On the one hand, they had this direction from Moses, but then they also had the statement in the book of Malachi. So, the question would have revealed a dilemma: "In which direction do we move?" Jesus comes down on the side of divorce being wrong.

But then, Jesus' disciples ask him to explain his answer further. His response is:

> "Anyone who divorces his wife and marries another woman commits adultery against her. And if she divorces her husband and marries another man, she commits adultery." (Mark 10:11–12)

If the most important thing to God is rules, then Jesus, it appears, is creating a new rule. One becomes an adulterer if one divorces and remarries. We are so convinced of this that we created the label—adulterer—as something we can stick onto people. Churches, Christians and pastors have done this for centuries, including, in some cases the refusal to marry people who divorce.

That perspective says that God hates us when we break the rules. But if God loves us and his point is healing, not punishment, like a mom whose son has burned his hand, then what it is telling us (both in Malachi and in Jesus' words) is that we are damaging ourselves, doing violence to ourselves. Our souls are damaged by divorce. What it is saying is that we will need to find healing from this trauma. It is telling us that God doesn't want us to go through that. Recognizing the damage of divorce should lead us into humility in seeing the damage done to our souls when we end friendships, exclude others, or cancel people. There is not a greater sin in one and a lesser sin in another. It is all damaging to our souls, and it is doing damage to other's souls. It all needs to be healed. This is why lust is like adultery. It damages the core of who we are. It deadens a part of us that should work.

That should lead the Church of Jesus to receive those who have been divorced, to comfort them and to aid them in recuperating. Rather than shunning and labeling them as people who don't and can never regain a place in God's love or in moving into a new relationship, we should be teaching them that they are surrounded by God's love. God's heart is as broken as theirs by this destruction in which they are living. In our desire to follow the rules, I discovered a church that would not bury a person who was divorced in their graveyard. An elderly Irish couple told me of their daughter who escaped an abusive marriage, divorced, and who was told that she was excluded from being married in the church as well as buried in the churchyard. They shared that a well-known gangster, a member of their village, who gave gifts to the church but otherwise was a known criminal was buried there, while daughter was kept out. They cried as they asked how that was possible, let alone fair to God. So, they were moving through life, while remaining in their church, with an ache and a sense of abandonment. Wouldn't that break God's heart as well?

The ancient story of creation of males and females in Gen 1, 2 and 3 includes the understanding that *humanity* (which is the meaning of the Hebrew word "adam") was made into two beings from one. It became male and female. That's why it says a husband will leave his parents, join his wife and they will become one being, with the sense of "*again*":

> That is why a man leaves his father and mother and is united to his
> wife, and they become one flesh. (Gen 2:24)

The core of the Genesis story is the value of each person—male and female—in our partnership in life and expresses the need we have as humanity to partner with each other equally. This concept echoes the creation statement of Gen 1, where God creates humanity in his image in Gen 1:27:

> So God created mankind in his own image,
> in the image of God he created them;
> male and female he created them.

We, of course, now touch the edge of the issue of gay marriage. Doesn't the symbolic expression of "oneness" now exclude homosexuals from marrying? It does if the most important thing to God is rules. If the most important thing to God is us, then God knows exactly what we feel, experience, and understand within ourselves. The couple that comes seeking to live in monogamy, caring for each other throughout their lives, comes before God in the same position as anyone else. The gay couple who desires to be part of lifelong commitment brings their flaws and damage into the commitment, just as any straight couple. Regardless of gender, we are valued and equal, and keeping each other's souls well is a responsibility we share. Jesus brings this understanding forward both here and in his own treatment of women. Paul echoes this when he writes in Gal 3:28:

There is neither Jew nor Gentile, neither slave nor free, nor is there male and female, for you are all one in Christ Jesus.

Men and women understand and experience life and the world differently, and so we need each other as partners—whether that includes marriage or members of the same community or business.

When a marriage is simply dismissed through a certificate or dismissed through an act of betrayal, there is a depth of damage to a soul that breaks God's heart. Jesus is not giving us another rule or law. He is describing the damage that is done to us when we separate, and the hurt God feels. Divorce is wrong because it does damage to our souls, not because it breaks a rule. The experience and reality of that damage is brought into any new relationship, and it will impact it. It will hurt to get remarried because we have to re-engage a level of relationship that was supposed to be there with another. We must know that walking in, so we can deal with it, clear it up with God's help, find healing, and grow from it: As the community of faith we should be extending grace to people who are remarrying, helping them to move through any grief or damage from a prior relationship into wholeness in this new one.

So, let me say again, I do realize that I am not speaking completely into the expressions of sexuality that we find in our world today. There is a whole community of people who feel excluded from God because of their sexual expressions, interests, and desires. When people realize that they don't fit with a typical bifurcated understanding of sexuality, they can feel or even be told that they don't fit with God. The thing that hurts God the most is when we use others rather than love them and help them see their own worth. The reality of sinfulness, the separation from God that we experience as human beings, is that any of us who desire to know and love God, and who accept redemption through the life and sacrifice of Jesus must seek to live in a manner that honors God and celebrates his grace. This challenges someone, anyone, who is using their sexuality for their own pleasure by using many partners without any commitment or ongoing care. This is just doing damage without thought. We don't dismiss these people. Instead, we seek to understand why they are living as they are, to care for them in their basic needs, and to provide them with any support we can offer. We encourage them to learn how to care for others, rather than making use of others.

However, the person, any person, who seeks to live in a monogamous relationship, honoring a partner with God, is the same as anyone else.

They're bringing themselves to God seeking grace and mercy like any other human being. Whether they choose celibacy or marriage, in seeking to honor God, the best the rest of us can do is to love them as they are. We live in a world that is confusing and damaging in many ways. Our best course, especially when we are struggling to find and live by truth, is to choose to love and to not do damage to another's soul. Choosing to shun, separate or dismiss the value of any of these brothers or sisters speaks against the work of Jesus in our own souls.

Jesus, in speaking into the breakdown of a relationship, talks to all of us about the care of souls.

> "You have heard that it was said, 'You shall not commit adultery.' But I tell you that anyone who looks at a woman lustfully has already committed adultery with her in his heart. If your right eye causes you to stumble, gouge it out and throw it away. It is better for you to lose one part of your body than for your whole body to be thrown into hell. And if your right hand causes you to stumble, cut it off and throw it away. It is better for you to lose one part of your body than for your whole body to go into hell.
> "It has been said, 'Anyone who divorces his wife must give her a certificate of divorce.' But I tell you that anyone who divorces his wife, except for sexual immorality, makes her the victim of adultery, and anyone who marries a divorced woman commits adultery. (Matt 5:27–32)

And then Jesus steps into speaking about promises, where we partner in life with someone in a manner that is less than marriage, but still involves our souls. He instructs his disciples that they will live in a different manner from those around them. They will not be people who try to find power or control in life from some idol, some feature of God, or some image of strength. Their strength will be based on their character or keeping their soul sound and whole. So, when they say "yes" or "no," it will mean what they said, and they will live in that direction:

> "Again, you have heard that it was said to the people long ago, 'Do not break your oath, but fulfill to the Lord the vows you have made.' But I tell you, do not swear an oath at all: either by heaven, for it is God's throne; or by the earth, for it is his footstool; or by Jerusalem, for it is the city of the Great King. And do not swear by your head, for you cannot make even one hair white or black. All you need to say is simply 'Yes' or 'No'; anything beyond this comes from the evil one. (Matt 5:33-37)

Jesus teaches these people that they have the same value as all those around them, and they need to remember the value others have that is equal to theirs. So, he then moves into living with others and what to do when things go wrong. He uses examples of life that all the people would understand, especially as they lived in a merchant society, seeking to buy and sell through the work of their hands and minds. When things break down in that society or when demands are made, his disciples are to be people who must seek to build wholeness in relationships and to recognize their own worth and express others' worth while doing that. The disciples of Jesus are not called to treat everyone else as having worth while not recognizing their own. It is out of their own worth that they are treat others as having the same worth.

So, he tells them to value the person more than the situation. More than winning in life, seek to win the heart of the other individual:

> "You have heard that it was said, 'Eye for eye, and tooth for tooth.' But I tell you, do not resist an evil person. If anyone slaps you on the right cheek, turn to them the other cheek also. And if anyone wants to sue you and take your shirt, hand over your coat as well. If anyone forces you to go one mile, go with them two miles. Give to the one who asks you, and do not turn away from the one who wants to borrow from you. (Matt 5:38–42)

He calls them into demonstrating their strength and the wholeness of their relationship with God. Our souls communicate and relate with God first. So, when someone slaps you, seeking to devalue you, allow them to strike you again so that they must make a choice. Give them the chance to recognize your worth alongside them. This includes even the Roman soldier who could force a Jewish person (any person really) to carry his pack for a mile. All the eyes around him would have opened wider to Jesus' words because they would know to whom he was referring. Even your enemies, even your oppressors have value. Even those people who would make use of you, the ones who treat you as if you only have the value of being used. When we go the extra mile, we demonstrate that we have value within ourselves; we are equal with the one who insults or demeans us. Their estimate of us does not express our value. We need to remember this as we read and experience the suffering Jesus goes through before and within the cross.

Jesus is teaching the value of every person on the planet including ourselves:

"You have heard that it was said, 'Love your neighbor and hate your enemy.' But I tell you, love your enemies and pray for those who persecute you, that you may be children of your Father in heaven. He causes his sun to rise on the evil and the good, and sends rain on the righteous and the unrighteous. If you love those who love you, what reward will you get? Are not even the tax collectors doing that? And if you greet only your own people, what are you doing more than others? Do not even pagans do that? (Matt 5:43–47)

This is so important to our culture at this moment. Because of the internet we can call down condemnation on someone who disagrees with us, has a completely alternative opinion on how life should be lived. We can create a mob of those who are on our side and move to damage them to the point of seeing them removed from their employment, their homes, and silencing their voice. We have the power to dismiss the value of any other being in our society with our typed words, in the same manner as pulling a trigger. Jesus' guidance is crucial for us to hear and to follow in this season of life. People are stopping debates over ideas and perspectives, not allowing others even to ask questions, as if their opinion is so fragile that any alternative must be screamed out of existence. And so, Jesus calls them to live as God does, with a mature perspective, to be the grown-up, to see the world not as someone who acts like a child, who thinks mostly about themselves and what they want or need and how they can get their way more than they think of the value and needs of the people around them. We translate this as "perfect," but the word carries the understanding and meaning of "mature": We have taught ourselves over and over that the thing people and God are looking for is perfection. It is so easy to fall into the trap of making "purity" the god we serve, rather than knowing and loving the One who understands life and is calling us to lean into his understanding.

"Be mature, therefore, as your heavenly Father is mature." (Matt 5:48)

Chapter Ten

How Should We Then Live?

JESUS NOW SHIFTS TO talking with his disciples about what is going on within them as they practice their faith or relationship with God. Within these words, he lays out a description of spiritual maturity and spiritual formation. This is what Christ followers should live like, act like, essentially, how they should become new as they live in relationship with God. They don't pretend. Under God's daily and even moment-by-moment guidance, they do what they can to establish the rightness that should be experienced by the people they meet. As Jesus continues talking he says they partner with God to bring wholeness to the world:

> "Be careful not to practice your righteousness in front of others to be seen by them. If you do, you will have no reward from your Father in heaven." (Matt 6:1)

When we think of a "reward from our Father in heaven," we can think Jesus means the reward will be heaven. We have equated heaven with salvation like it's an end result, like we get paradise for being good. This is what religions and some expressions of Christianity all over the world and the Pharisees expected. But Jesus is speaking about the present moment throughout this passage.

The idea of reward, which can also be translated as "pay" or "wage," is more like *benefit*. It is something good and tangible that we will receive now. If we continue to think in terms of maturity, like God is mature, then one benefit would be growth in maturity. Our stability, wisdom, inner strength are all benefits that grow as we act quietly, rather than so others can see us, so that we are working with God in bringing healing and wholeness to others. We become more capable and more in touch with God, more able to recognize God's Spirit when God is speaking to us. We are maturing in our souls.

Soul work is tangible reality to Jesus. A reward or benefit that comes to us from God enhances life now. This corresponds to how we diminish our connection with God when we deaden some aspect of our souls in sin. When we choose death, separation from others, dismissing the worth of others, lording it over others and we deaden or cut off a line of communication between us and God, we are diminished in our ability to live well. Jesus is calling us to abundant life, and he knows that the inner "benefit" of growth, connection, insight, and wisdom leads into an abundance that can be shared.

There's a good possibility, in this next part of the Sermon on the Mount, that Jesus made up a word that we use all the time—hypocrite. This is the Greek word for "actor." Jesus may have used it in a new way as he spoke. A small city called Sepphoris was being built just four to five miles away from Nazareth, Jesus' hometown, throughout his lifetime. One of its features was a theater. Joseph, Jesus' adoptive dad, was a "tekton," a word we have traditionally translated as "carpenter," but is more like a construction worker. This was a person who could make you something out of stone, like walls, could make you something out of wood, like a door, and could make you something out of metal, like the hinges . . . a construction worker. Jesus was a construction worker like his dad we are told, and throughout his childhood and early adulthood Sepphoris would be a place of ready employment. It would have been natural for Jesus to see actors— "hypocrites"—on the street, going to work, calling attention to themselves. As far as we know, it does not seem like people used this word the way Jesus does in this passage before him. He tells his disciples, don't be like people who pretend:

> "So when you give to the needy, do not announce it with trumpets, as the hypocrites (actors) do in the synagogues and on the streets, to be honored by others. Truly I tell you, they have received their reward in full. But when you give to the needy, do not let your left hand know what your right hand is doing, so that your giving may be in secret. Then your Father, who sees what is done in secret, will reward you." (Matt 6:2-4)

Whatever we do, we are to do it with God and to do it without bringing notice to ourselves or our actions when we are around other people. Whether it is providing financial aid, praying, fasting, whatever, we are not to do it so others will take note and form an opinion of us through that. If we display ourselves, other people's opinion is the only benefit we will receive and that cuts us off from our relationship with them, with those we help, and with God. Instead of acting justly, fairly and equally with others, we are placing ourselves in a position to be admired above others. We gain nothing other than someone being impressed with us for a bit. The one with whom we are to connect is God who sees everything we do:

> "And when you pray, do not be like the hypocrites, for they love to pray standing in the synagogues and on the street corners to be seen by others. Truly I tell you, they have received their reward in full. But when you pray, go into your room, close the door and pray to your Father, who is unseen. Then your Father, who sees what is done in secret, will reward you. And when you pray, do not keep on babbling like pagans, for they think they will be heard because of their many words. Do not be like them, for your Father knows what you need before you ask him.
> "This, then, is how you should pray:
> "'Our Father in heaven,
> hallowed be your name,
> your kingdom come,
> your will be done,
> on earth as it is in heaven.
> Give us today our daily bread.
> And forgive us our debts,
> as we also have forgiven our debtors.
> And lead us not into temptation,
> but deliver us from the evil one.
> For if you forgive other people when they sin against you, your heavenly Father will also forgive you. But if you do not forgive others their sins, your Father will not forgive your sins.
> "When you fast, do not look somber as the hypocrites do, for they disfigure their faces to show others they are fasting. Truly I tell you, they have received their reward in full. But when you fast, put oil on your head and wash your face, so that it will not be obvious to others that you are fasting, but only to your Father, who is unseen; and your Father, who sees what is done in secret, will reward you." (Matt 6:5-18)

The Lord's Prayer that we have in the midst of this passage has enough books written analyzing it, so I just want to lift up a couple of things. The first is the basis it gives to relationship. Jesus was not the first or only person to refer to God as Father or Father in heaven. He distinctively used the term "Abba" during his ministry, which caught the attention of his followers and which they mimicked and taught to those who came after them. "Abba" is a more conversational and intimate name for Father, but it is not what Jesus uses here. He uses the word "pater," but even with this he draws his followers into the understanding that God is not someone distant but someone immediate. God is engaged here with us.

The other element I would like to focus on is forgiveness. There are many understandings of the word "forgive," but the one I like best is "choosing not to punish someone who is guilty." Because we have the phrase "forgive and forget," we have tied forgiveness into the idea of forgetting. It is a nice idea, but forgiving is not about forgetting. It does not pretend that someone is not guilty. Forgiving is about not tying our relationship with them to that incident. The Greek word for "forgiving" carries the sense of releasing or loosing. We are told to release others from what they "owe" us, or how they diminished us, or how they have taken a chunk out of our hide in one way or another. Instead, we are to set them free of the obligation to pay us back, free to find life that doesn't use or abuse others. We also don't have to "get them back" for what they did to us. We can move ahead freely.

There have been times in my life when I learned, because of the damage someone did to me, that I could be a friend to them, but they could not be a friend to me. It seemed clear to me that I would not be able to trust them again, at least not for a while, but I could remain trustworthy towards them. As it happens, there have been moments when I was thrown back into making a choice in how I treat them. Once, I had to perform a wedding for a family where one of the participants was someone who had damaged me and those I loved deeply. I worked hard to include them in the ceremony as I would with any member of the family, which would put them in the best light. At the end of the time, this person approached me and thanked me for my words and actions. It was in going through that experience that I learned how I could still act as a friend with someone who could no longer be that to me. Doing that with prayer, recognizing my need for God's presence and guidance, taught my soul that this was possible, helpful and life-giving for everyone, including myself. We may not forget, but we don't have to punish.

On the other hand, and part of amazing grace, God does indeed forget our sins. We're told that he throws our sins into a ocean, to the depths of the sea (Mic 7:19). Since God does this, shouldn't we when we are able? Not holding something against someone is the essence of forgiveness. God is capable of doing more than we can, not simply forgiving but also wiping out of existence what we've done. A greater depth of forgiveness than we can manage in our own strength. We may remember what was done to us, and we don't have to live pretending it isn't there or didn't hurt. We may even need distance between us and those whom we forgive. None of that precludes us from choosing not to punish them. Being safe from those who might damage us doesn't mean we haven't forgiven them.

When we think of the story of the prodigal son and how he came back to his father, whom he shamed in front of their family and their community, whom he treated as worthless to himself, he asks to pay his father back. He asks to be a servant in his father's household and to never be recognized again as a son. He is willing to spend his life paying his father back, but that wasn't what the father wanted. This was not the way of the father in the story, and Jesus tells us it is not the way of our Father in heaven.

We cannot actually come up with any means of paying God back for our disrespect and dishonesty when we act like he is not in the world or does not matter to us, and God is not looking for that. He is looking to be merciful. He is looking to shower us with grace and to build up peace and strength within us. He is looking to heal us. God is seeking for a maturing within our spirits that comes through our accepting God's love, recognition of the damage we caused, taking responsibility, admitting the damage, and even making amends with a person we've harmed in some way. From there, God knows what being merciful will do within us when we forgive, that it will heal and mature us, and God calls us to share in that experience. So, he calls us to forgive, to release someone who does us wrong, to set them free.

Our son, Sam, was always watching for my car when it was pick-up time at his preschool. If he didn't see the car in the first three in line at the end of the day he started crying. I finally stopped getting into line and bypassed it, driving into the parking lot, parking and walking in to get Sam. But one day my car just wouldn't start, so I ran to Sam's school. It was only a quarter mile, but still, I was going to be late. I came running into his classroom and he was standing there, calm as could be, ready to go. We walked back to where I had left my car, and halfway there, I started to apologize and explain what happened and why I was late. He stops, puts up his hand to stop me from talking, and says, "It's okay, Dad." But, then he starts shrugging off his backpack, zipping it open and digging inside. We're just standing on the side of the road when he pulls this slip of paper out of his bag. Turns out, it was part of a very timely lesson in preschool. It read: "This is your free Second Chance coupon. Use it well and then pass it on to someone who needs it." "That's for you, Dad," Sam said, "it's okay!" I felt free indeed.

Jesus calls his followers into having generous spirits. We have been given everything. We have been given new lives in rest. We need to offer that to those around us but especially to those who have mistreated us because something has deadened within them. We are to call them back to life, just as God does with us. As we do that and as it is accepted and lived into, the deadening that was within the other person's soul can come back to life, as it came back to life within us. So, Jesus uses the terms of finance to express all this. Think how this would speak to people around him, who were living hand to mouth, having to find food every day, to create a livelihood, to pay taxes, to figure from scratch how to cover losses from weather, oppression or carelessness.

Why would Jesus use rewards or wages, debts, treasure as the elements by which he illustrated his points? It's because money has spiritual power. It affects our souls. I believe Jesus did this because money is the closest thing we have to the power of God. Money gets things done. We can make something happen when we have money. It is a power that we put in the face of God.

Jesus is using this part of our lives, on which we focus so intently, to get us thinking about the power of God to change life. He calls us to lift up the eyes of our souls to recognize the present power of God to make life better, more than money can. He then uses a colloquialism about generosity to bring us even closer to the idea. If the eyes of our souls are focused on money, if that is where we believe power actually resides by the way we act, think, and live, then our eyes are not healthy. Our souls are dark because our eyes are dark, clouded over with an assurance of power that is not lasting or real. It is a power we end up serving, enslaved to, which demands more and more work. We are to have generous spirits, with healthy eyes that see the power of God moving in the world:

> "Do not store up for yourselves treasures on earth, where moths
> and vermin destroy, and where thieves break in and steal. But store
> up for yourselves treasures in heaven, where moths and vermin do

not destroy, and where thieves do not break in and steal. For where your treasure is, there your heart will be also.

"The eye is the lamp of the body. If your eyes are healthy, your whole body will be full of light. But if your eyes are unhealthy, your whole body will be full of darkness. If then the light within you is darkness, how great is that darkness!" (Matt 6:19–23)

Jesus lays this out plainly then. We are either going to be part of life with God or we are going to serve the demands of money. Money has a place in life. It is a tool to use as we seek to bring healing to the world. But, if we use it for control of life, to take care of ourselves and not to bring healing and wholeness into other lives, then we are serving it. It is not serving us. And when we serve money, then we have all the anxiety that comes with having, needing, and wanting money:

> "No one can serve two masters. Either you will hate the one and love the other, or you will be devoted to the one and despise the other. You cannot serve both God and money. Therefore I tell you, do not worry about your life, what you will eat or drink; or about your body, what you will wear. Is not life more than food, and the body more than clothes? Look at the birds of the air; they do not sow or reap or store away in barns, and yet your heavenly Father feeds them. Are you not much more valuable than they? Can any one of you by worrying add a single hour to your life? "And why do you worry about clothes? See how the flowers of the field grow. They do not labor or spin. Yet I tell you that not even Solomon in all his splendor was dressed like one of these. If that is how God clothes the grass of the field, which is here today and tomorrow is thrown into the fire, will he not much more clothe you—you of little faith? So do not worry, saying, 'What shall we eat?' or 'What shall we drink?' or 'What shall we wear?' For the pagans run after all these things, and your heavenly Father knows that you need them. But seek first his kingdom and his righteousness, and all these things will be given to you as well. Therefore do not worry about tomorrow, for tomorrow will worry about itself. Each day has enough trouble of its own." (Matt 6:24–34)

Worry is pretending to do something. It uses up our time and energy, but it doesn't accomplish anything. When we seek the power of money over the power of God, we separate ourselves from God's presence, and we lean onto worrying, aching for safety. We start looking out for ourselves, to make ourselves and the care of ourselves more important than anyone or anything else. The more we worry over finding and making money, the more we begin to eliminate the value of others. We begin to decide the worth of someone else by what they can provide or do for us, and in what way they measure up in *our* world. If we live this way, then we will begin to deaden our souls. Instead of worrying, we need to look at their need and our measuring up to meet that need. If we don't, we become actors, pretenders, just like a Pharisee:

> "Do not judge, or you too will be judged. For in the same way you judge others, you will be judged, and with the measure you use, it will be measured to you. Why do you look at the speck of sawdust in your brother's eye and pay no attention to the plank in your own eye? How can you say to your brother, 'Let me take the speck out of your eye,' when all the time there is a plank in your own eye? You hypocrite, first take the plank out of your own eye, and then you will see clearly to remove the speck from your brother's eye." (Matt 7:1-5)

Discovering the worth we all have, our worth and the worth of other people are the foundation of spiritual formation, God's shaping us into being like Christ. So, we are called to learn people, not to judge them. At the same time, we do need to be watchful toward sharing what God does within our souls with other people who are not in any way focused on that. We want to live the truth of it out to them and around them, instead of trying to argue them into believing in Jesus or God, which could seem like an act of judgment, a "holier than thou" attitude. That will backfire. As we live into the way of life Jesus teaches us, we are to live it simply, plainly to others, mostly without talking about it. If we try to take the deep lessons and experiences we gain from God's work in our souls, and try to bring that into the lives of people who are living at the level of day-to-day survival with sermons and lectures, we aren't paying attention to the value of what we've learned, what it's taken for us to understand it, nor the value of people with whom we want to share it.

It will be experienced as if we are putting them down, rather than seeking to bring wholeness into their lives. It won't offer them anything they can use. Or, it can be experienced as simple stupidity, that is getting in the way of how they know life must work, and it would be natural for them to turn on us:

> "Do not give dogs what is sacred; do not throw your pearls to pigs.
> If you do, they may trample them under their feet, and turn and
> tear you to pieces." (Matt 7:6)

So, instead of getting consumed within our souls with how other people should change, we are to focus on partnering with God in bringing wholeness, peace, and rightness to the world. We can get waylaid with all the damage we see around us, with the way other people are separating themselves from God and hurting the world and others. We can get consumed in trying to change them to the point of trying to create laws to make them do what we know they "should" be doing. This is simply living into fear and worry. It is making fear a god we must serve, seeking to find some power that will make us feel safer. We can get lost in political efforts to make life run the way we demand it to run, rather than intentionally bringing healing to the people who are most ready for healing. We need to find the people in whom God's Spirit has been working, so we can join with him in creating the rightness they should find in life.

Think of the choice of God in sending Jesus to us. Jesus could have been sent to the king of Israel, the Emperor of Rome, to the rich and powerful. He could have been sent to get in the faces of those who seek to control and dominate, who are crushing hopes and dreams by demanding that life work for them the way they want it to work. He might even have convinced them that he was everything he is, but, then, they would have used the tools they understood on how to get people to act in the way they wanted . . . power and control. Think of Constantine simply making everyone "Christian" in his domain, when he decided that this was the way to go. Instead, Jesus is sent in the lowliest of manners, to a working family, to go through the whole process of growing up, and to a people who were ready to hear words of healing and wholeness. He sits down with those who were judged and who would understand themselves as sinners. He eats with them. And, when he is challenged about doing that, he explains that he is coming like a physician to those who know that something isn't working right inside them.

Keep this thought going. Recall a doctor who takes you seriously when you are not feeling well. Now imagine how you would feel if they didn't listen or if they treated you briskly, or even as if your explanation of what you are dealing with is not important. Suppose the doctor treated you as if they already knew everything there was to know about you and your situation and just handed you a prescription. When a doctor takes us seriously, when they pay attention, it helps us to take their wisdom seriously. Along with Jesus, bringing the healing power of God into the lives of others means that we are to recognize our own limitations, and how we might identify with those we are sent to help because they are just like us.

Most of the people with whom Jesus came in contact were ready for an alternative to what they were living. He came to them as one of them. Some of us are called by God to go to a foreign land to share his good news with people whose culture and language we'll have to learn. Most of us, however, need to look at our own community, the people of our neighborhood, the type of people we're like and whom we know. These are the people Jesus came to first, the people who lived life as he did. These were the ones who had received the promises and words of God, who already would understand the God about whom he spoke and who he was there to reveal in depth. It will be enough of a challenge for most of us, to live a Christ-centered life with those who are like us. That will be the kind of experience that will drive us into truly seeing our limitations. That will turn us back to God for strength, help, and guidance.

Think of how many times we are told that Jesus stepped off to talk life over with God. Did he do that so he could hear what to do? Did he do that to keep his partnership with God clearly before him, teaching his soul how dependent he was, as one of us, on the relationship he had with God the Father and God the Holy Spirit? We have the same opportunity. We have the opportunity Jesus had to continually walk back into the fullness of relationship with God and to depend on that. As we do that, we will find answers and help. We will find that God loves us more than we imagine and understands what we are dealing with in the world. We will find that God wants to provide us with what we need:

> "Ask and it will be given to you; seek and you will find; knock and the door will be opened to you. For everyone who asks receives; the one who seeks finds; and to the one who knocks, the door will be opened.
> "Which of you, if your son asks for bread, will give him a stone? Or if he asks for a gifts to your children, how much more will your Father in heaven give good gifts to those who ask him! (Matt 7:7–9)

We are not to live for ourselves but to live for and to express the value of every person in the world including ourselves:

> So in everything, do to others what you would have them do to you, for this sums up the Law and the Prophets. (Matt 7:12)

Obviously, this is not going to be the most profitable, popular, or easiest way to live. Living under the guidance of the instructions of God will make others belittle or seek to take advantage of us. But we are still to live that way because that is how the world was created to work, in partnership with God. This is what brings life rather than death to the world:

> "Enter through the narrow gate. For wide is the gate and broad is the road that leads to destruction, and many enter through it. But small is the gate and narrow the road that leads to life, and only a few find it. (Matt 7:13–14)

And as we live this way, there will be people who will seek to make a profit off it. They will come seeking power or attention, while trying to act as if they are part of the community of Jesus' followers. Over and over, Jesus calls his first disciples away from the kinds of choices that focused on gaining personal power or position. And here, he tells them to watch for people who get the manner of life he is living and those who are just acting. He tells his disciples how to recognize these kinds of people:

> "Watch out for false prophets. They come to you in sheep's clothing, but inwardly they are ferocious wolves. By their fruit you will recognize them. Do people pick grapes from thornbushes, or figs from thistles? Likewise, every good tree bears good fruit, but a bad tree bears bad fruit. A good tree cannot bear bad fruit, and a bad tree cannot bear good fruit. Every tree that does not bear good fruit is cut down and thrown into the fire. Thus, by their fruit you will recognize them. (Matt 7:15–19)

There are always people who believe they can mix the instructions of God with the fulfillment of their desires. Jesus calls us away from any pretense. We are not actors figuring out how to best portray a part or image. We are to be genuine, allowing the instructions of God to infiltrate our souls. We see the downfall of those who tried to create positions of authority, and to take advantage of that authority in the lives of those who trust them, instead of using their positions, power, and authority to create opportunities for healing. Whether they are politicians or pastors, they separate themselves from the presence and power of God and become actors without substance. They have their total reward now. There's no more after this:

> "Not everyone who says to me, 'Lord, Lord,' will enter the kingdom of heaven, but only the one who does the will of my Father who is in heaven. Many will say to me on that day, 'Lord, Lord, did we not prophesy in your name and in your name drive out demons and in your name perform many miracles?' Then I will tell them plainly, 'I never knew you. Away from me, you evildoers!' (Matt 7:21–23)

Jesus sums up this call to sincerity in life with an image that speaks in ultimate terms. The point of his wisdom is to put it into action. Wisdom isn't wisdom until it is used. It isn't some catchy phrase we can needlepoint and frame to hang on a wall. If we nod our heads and agree, "Yup . . . that's a good idea. That's the way people should live," then it's just an idea. It doesn't really touch anything. If it remains just that, then we can live for a while feeling secure, but, when life in all its reality crashes down on us, we will be lost:

> "Therefore everyone who hears these words of mine and puts them into practice is like a wise man who built his house on the rock. The rain came down, the streams rose, and the winds blew and beat against that house; yet it did not fall, because it had its foundation on the rock. But everyone who hears these words of mine and does not put them into practice is like a foolish man who built his house on sand. The rain came down, the streams rose, and the winds blew and beat against that house, and it fell with a great crash." (Matt 7:24-29)

Like the owners of the houses still standing in the midst of devastation in Florida and in Southern California, we can follow the guidance and instructions that are available, or we can just try to make the world bend to our will.

Chapter Eleven

Making the Most of It

WHAT'S THE POINT? WHAT'S the point of recognizing that God gave instructions for life and how to be human to the people at Mount Sinai? What's the point of hearing that Jesus is God's tone of voice? What's the point of living into the wisdom and call of Jesus in our lives?

First, we get rid of the list. We must stop reading, learning, or even creating our own additional commandments for being good. The point is not about being good according to a list. The point is to find God's healing in our own life, to learn to recognize God's voice in our own soul, and then to partner with God in living life well by bringing wholeness and healing into others' lives right around us. The point is not being good. The point is being alive for the benefit of others.

Maybe making a list of commandments or trying to be perfect isn't your deal. Maybe you're fine in your opinion and you don't see the point of "religion." Why add religion into your life when you're doing pretty good as you are?

Jesus calls us into something deeper than religion. He calls us into a relationship with God, the creator of all, that is not based on being good but on being involved in life every day, with the worth of every person naturally recognized and responded to, and with recognizing God as intimately present and proactively engaged with the world. He calls us into knowing we don't know everything, and, remarkably, learning that religion is not an answer. At its best, it is simply a means of reminding ourselves that there is wisdom we don't have or can get just on our own. It must come from God and God desires to share it with us daily. Being part of a church, a community of faith, when it opens the doorways for that to happen, is a celebration of that truth. A church community can guide us to the tools that will help us to learn and grow. Essentially, Jesus calls us into being spiritually formed so we can partner with God in healing the world. Through this we learn that God's will is not a "plan." It's about living in a relationship.

When I was in college and people around me were talking about "God's will for their life," they were talking about it as a plan. They could have substituted the word "plan" for "will." They kept trying to discover "What's God's plan for my life?" As they continued talking in that way, what was troubling them most of all was a fear of not figuring out God's plan. They were praying to get it right on a regular basis and worrying over getting it wrong. What if they chose someone to marry or a career path that wasn't God's will? What if they went through the next couple of decades in a relationship or following a course of study and employment and it turned out that God had a different design for them completely.

Of course, one of the interesting moments was when a guy came to a girl and told her that, in his prayers, he learned that she was God's will for his life. That was really interesting for the girl who hadn't heard the same thing about him in her prayers. The fear that "my life could go off on a tangent from what God intended" just stymied some people. That kind of attitude, revealed in those words, showed they weren't going to God to ask for guidance daily or even moment by moment. They weren't seeking to know God. They were seeking control over a sense of chaos, the "not knowing" how the future will play out. They needed to find guidance that would have a controlled outcome, to show a particular way of life, and to fulfill a certain destiny. They were sure there was a plan and that the Christian's job was to figure out the plan so they could be "in God's will."

This was just another aspect of being "pure." If they could land on the line that was God's will and remain perfect in staying on the line, they would have the outcome they most desired from life . . . God's love and heaven. It's also another way of seeing God as just a big human being who must keep everything under control.

What if God's will was simple like . . .

> He has shown you, O mortal, what is good. And what does
> the Lord require of you? To act justly and to love mercy and to
> walk humbly with your God. (Mic 6:8)

Rejoice always, pray continually, give thanks in all circumstances; for this is God's will for you in Christ Jesus. (1 Thess 5:16–18)

What if God's will is both general and specific? There is a certain way or manner in which we are to live, and there are moments when God will speak into our souls to tell us he wants us to act, to act now in a particular way. I was on a plane flying back home and had a stop over in Charlotte, North Carolina. There were only two seats in my row, and a young woman took the seat next to me. When the flight attendants came by asking if we'd like a beverage, she ordered three Bloody Mary mixes and vodkas. She paid for them, and they were delivered. Two she had right then, and one mix and bottle of vodka was stowed away in her purse for later. As we flew, she pulled out the most detailed astrological charts and journal I'd ever seen. My background had led me into magic and exploring sorcery, as I was seeking control over life. I knew what she was looking at and looking for.

In a very clear manner, I heard the Spirit of God direct me to talk with her. Without speaking out loud I said "no" just as plainly. This didn't feel like a good situation in any way. I didn't want to get involved. The prompt from the Spirit came again: "Speak to her." And just as plainly I answered, "no." Then she folded everything up and stored them in the seat pocket and I told the Spirit, "See . . . it would be very odd for me to bring it up since she put it away." Within three or four minutes, she pulled everything back out again. The prompt came again. So, I sighed, asked for help, thought for a moment and asked, "So, are you into astrology for fun or for the benefits?" She looked up smiling and said, "Oh, definitely for the benefits." "Really," I said, "Tell me about that."

She proceeded to explain to me the way that all of the stars, movements, alignments, and groupings provided helpful information for her. I knew a lot of what she was talking about, but I asked a number of questions for clarity. She shared how she did readings of the stars for herself and family and friends to help them or to guide them to anticipate issues that could arise in the future. Then she asked, "Are you into astrology?" I said, "No . . . no . . . I'm into God." And she said, "Tell me about that."

I told her about giving up my desire to control life and to seek to hear and understand God's voice. I explained that I paid attention to God daily, even moment by moment, to learn what God wanted me to do. I did admit that sometimes I wasn't as good at it as I wanted to be, but I kept trying. After a bit, answering questions she brought up, she said, "So, you're saying . . . people can have a personal relationship with God." I nodded and said,

"That's a good way to describe it," and I added, "I think that's the way Jesus lived it out and explained it." That led into a conversation about Jesus, who he was, how he cleared the way for people to hear God again, the way they were created, and how he cleared away the illness from souls that we call sin.

The plane was landing and our conversation almost ended there. She asked if I was staying in Charlotte and I explained I was catching another plane. She then told me that she was coming back because she had gotten a DUI and had to appear in court later. She was staying with her grandparents. I couldn't help but think how she'd already finished two Bloody Mary's before 9AM, and she was headed to a judge about a DUI. Life was pretty out of control for this young woman. I told her I'd be praying for her and that things would work out. She thanked me and, as we were already off the plane, we parted.

I trust that God's will was for that young woman to learn of a God with whom she could have a personal relationship. I trust that God desired to use me to tell her about Jesus in a manner she could hear and consider. I trust that God was clearing the way for someone else to talk into her heart, so that she could come to God through Jesus and discover a life free from seeking control through means beyond alcohol or the stars. God's will is for us to be free and not enslaved to anything.

Paul was a person who knew ... *knew* ... that God had a certain way for his people to live. His life as a Pharisee, as I wrote before, was built on keeping the law, of essentially being a slave. But when he heard the message of life from a resurrected Jesus, Paul rejected all forms of slavery, not obedience that grew out of love and relationship and partnership, but the one that was a slavery that grew out of a commandment, and the belief that God was only interested in rules.

The book of Galatians, one of the earliest books of our New Testament, speaks to the heart of Paul's conviction that God never wanted us to live in demanded obedience. He speaks to a group of gentile (non-Jewish) people about how they are being tricked into becoming slaves again. He is astounded, as he begins the letter, that they can't see that.

As the early Christian church developed, there was a certain group of followers of Jesus who believed that the only people getting into heaven were the Jews. Gentiles could get in, secondarily, but they needed to become as close to Jewish regulations before that could happen, if at all. We read about these people at various moments in Paul's letters, but, very clearly, we find them in the book of Galatians.

Paul reminds the Galatians that they were "enslaved" by the elemental forces of the world before they came to know Jesus. They had given themselves over to worshiping the power of control by worshiping the various gods who represented these forces. Some people believe these are demons or devils, but the point is that they are elemental forces that seem to provide control until they control us. Paul is showing the Galatians that if they fall into the trap of seeking a contractual relationship with the God promoted by the people infiltrating their community, they will be enslaved again. We read in Gal 4:8–9,

> Formerly, when you did not know God, you were slaves to those who by nature are not gods. But now that you know God—or rather are known by God—how is it that you are turning back to those weak and miserable forces? Do you wish to be enslaved by them all over again?

He goes on to challenge them to hang on to the freedom found in Christ. The people who were challenging them to keep the Jewish laws, were saying that all the men had to be circumcised, according to Jewish custom. In Gal 5:1–6, Paul contrasts this requirement, this "contract" with God, to the justice and grace found in living with Jesus:

> It is for freedom that Christ has set us free. Stand firm, then, and do not let yourselves be burdened again by a yoke of slavery.
> Mark my words! I, Paul, tell you that if you let yourselves be circumcised, Christ will be of no value to you at all. Again I declare to every man who lets himself be circumcised that he is obligated to obey the whole law. You who are trying to be justified by the law have been alienated from Christ; you have fallen away from grace. For through the Spirit we eagerly await by faith the righteousness for which we hope. For in Christ Jesus neither circumcision nor uncircumcision has any value. The only thing that counts is faith expressing itself through love.

This is part of the work Paul did in helping people to find their way into freedom and life. When we read in 1 Thess 5:16–18 that God's will for us is to rejoice always, pray continually, and to give thanks in all situations . . . doesn't this sound like wisdom on how to live?

As we walk through life with Jesus, we begin to see that God's will is not a plan, it is a conversation, which is the real idea behind "praying continually." The very essence of spiritual formation is a continual conversation that goes on every day, throughout the day. The essence of spiritual formation is listening to God and talking life over with God and getting shaped by the conversation. I admit again that sometimes I'm stubborn and am afraid of being embarrassed, but I've found that life works better when I'm following through on what I'm told I should do.

Giving up law and learning to listen plainly to God is difficult for a lot of people. I was invited to come to an evening gathering of atheists for some dessert, wine, and conversation about God and the Bible. It turned out to be a fascinating conversation because I could not move these people who didn't believe in God into an understanding of the freedom we find in Jesus. They brought up this verse, 1 Thess 5:17, "pray continually," asking how that was possible.

I made the point, with gentle sarcasm I admit, that it obviously wasn't about getting on one's knees and praying to God twenty-four hours a day. They didn't get the joke. They said, "But that's what it says." So, I became explicit, that this wasn't the idea of the words. The idea was a conversation. It was a prompt to talk with God all the time since God is right here with us, always. They argued that I was missing the point, and that it was simply a ridiculous requirement toward piety.

I again, smiling, suggested in the context of the letter of Thessalonians that Paul was writing to encourage them to live lives of integrity and faith, knowing that God was caring for them in the deepest of ways. People had come to Thessalonica suggesting that Christians who died before Jesus returned weren't saved. Paul assures them of God's love and that these people who died were now held by God. He calls on them to live into the will of God which would be seen in their rejoicing always, talking with God all the time and living the fullness of gratitude. All of these were expressions of their confidence in God's presence with them now and after they died. Paul is assuring them that none of those who died were in jeopardy. The dessert party of atheists would have none of it. Praying continually was a requirement.

They couldn't hear that the guidance in Paul's words here is that we give up the search for God's will or plan or a contract relationship with requirements and seek to listen to the God who is speaking to us every day, nor to grow into spiritual health through repeated gratitude. They couldn't hear that the single and most crucial difference between us and Jesus was not some sort of "goodness." It was being in communication with God. Jesus was never separated from God, never disconnected. When it says that Jesus "never sinned" and that he "knew no sin," it means that his lines of communication were never cut. He never made a choice that killed off some part of himself that should work. We can be in communication with God, and we can follow the pattern of Jesus, but this isn't a plan. It's part of the joy-filled and thankful conversation with God that can permeate every day.

There's an old pastor's story that needs to be addressed here. When we see Jesus on the cross, one of the statements he makes is "my God, my God, why have you forsaken me." I have heard this described as the one moment when all communication lines went down between Jesus and God. The way I have heard it said most is that God the Father turned his back on Jesus because he couldn't allow himself to see the "sin" that Jesus became. In other words, Jesus became so bad by receiving all the sin of the world that God turned his back on his only Son.

What this means, if we play it out, is that God could also turn his back on us. We just need to be bad enough. God's love stops. God's heart is no longer turned toward us because God hates us for being bad, or that we've crossed some line. This idea of God turning away from Jesus, when he is on the cross, means that the most important thing to God is the rules and all the punishment for all the broken rules comes down on Jesus.

This isn't the nature of God. It's the nature of human beings. We're told that nothing stops the love of God in Rom 8:38–39:

> For I am convinced that neither death nor life, neither angels nor demons, neither the present nor the future, nor any powers, neither height nor depth, nor anything else in all creation, will be able to separate us from the love of God that is in Christ Jesus our Lord.

Jesus was the only person on the planet or in history who never lost contact with God. Jesus was quoting a psalm on the cross, Ps 22, which begins in tragedy with the words, ". . . why have you forsaken me" and ends with triumph. The other psalm (Ps 31) that Jesus quotes when he says, "Into your hands I commit my spirit. . ." is again a psalm that begins with despair and need and ends with triumph and hope. In no place does the Bible say that God turned away from Jesus, because it didn't happen. This was made up by people who were working desperately hard to be and to remain pure. They were sure that this was Jesus' objective and example as well, that he was pure. Whole lives, deep and determined efforts have been given over to the god of "purity."

WAS IT ALL A WASTE?

When we think of the Bible as the history of people getting God wrong, we can think that all the effort of generations of people trying to keep rules was useless. What about the Jews who built practices of strict obedience over centuries? What about Christians who still try as they have for centuries to become pure or made vast sacrifices or claims on behalf of God that led to shunning family members or departures from advancement in society? What about those who gave up everything to live in monasteries or to never marry? What about all the efforts, practices, communities, and rules that were put into place just to demonstrate adherence to God?

Who are we to condemn or challenge another's heart in their seeking after God? We are not called to judge others, but to seek after God. We are not the know-it-alls who are the only ones who get God right.

Although there was damage and destruction, sometimes horrific and inexcusable, by people who chose these routes, there were also grand and glorifying results experienced as people attempted to give themselves over to God by those strict practices of obedience. We should not deny the good while fearlessly admitting when trauma crashed in on life, done by people of similar persuasions, sometimes. Art, wisdom, lifetimes of service all are part of our history because of people who sought to hang on to a sense of being unworthy of grace, but to live with an expectation of that grace being discovered someday after death. We should honor the hearts that were given away to God by searching out those practices and seeking to understand them, even if we are deeply ashamed of what was chosen by some of those who also followed these practices. Not every Pharisee was an enemy of Jesus. Some came seeking to grow in his light.

While we cannot deny the genocides, the power struggles from the self-absorption, the tragic demands for obedience to hierarchical structures or Scriptural interpretations that led to broken lives and hearts, we can admit to those without claiming that there were some who lived in a similar perception of God but with a rightness that benefited the community around them. We can also try to explore what was gained within practices by people of past ages. There were people who followed these practices into a depth of faith and understanding. There were others who followed the same practices into self-righteousness and the destruction of people's spirits and lives. The practice isn't to blame. Praying on a street corner to demonstrate one's piety and praying in a closed room away from all but God is still praying. The benefit of the time may not be experienced, but the people doing it may have felt like they were doing what they were taught to do. The choices and hearts of people who exaggerated the implications toward purity within the practices led them into destruction and separation.

But now, we are to avoid doing the same kinds of things. We aren't to seek after political power to hold people in check. We aren't to seek after control of others. We are to demonstrate to them the benefit and life-giving experience of knowing and loving God. We're to make friends with people who are different, to listen to their fears and struggles, to learn the nature of the control they seek and to provide alternatives. The question then is, how do we do that? How do we turn ourselves over fully to God and allow God to make the path work for us?

Chapter Twelve

Clay in the Potter's Hands

> But now, O Lord, you are our Father;
>> we are the clay, and you are our potter;
>> we are all the work of your hand. (Isa 64:8)

HUMBLING OURSELVES TO GOD'S understanding and avoiding leaning into our own makes us pliable to God's Spirit. Jesus told his disciples that the Spirit would come upon them and take up residence within them. The Spirit would be with them, just as he had been with his earliest disciples. When the Spirit is planted within us, it grows in strength and begins to shape our character. We change and our desire to change does as well. We get changed by the one with whom we spend the most time, the one who loves us and whom we love.

I had a couple in one church where I served whose daughter was born with a severe illness. She was just a tiny thing when I went to visit them all in the hospital. The father greeted me outside the area where she was being kept, a pediatric ICU. He explained to me that we were going to wash our hands before we went in. He led me to sinks that were right there, and I washed my hands. As I stood straight to grab a paper towel, he stopped me. "We're not done yet." He then went on to explain how else we were going to clean our hands, the time we were going to spend, the cleanliness under nails, in between our fingers. He showed me, as he did all this, that we were not going to have any possibility of bringing any kind of germs into the life of this little person he adored. He said, "It's not a matter of the temperature of the water that gets you clean. It's the time you spend with the soap."

Change comes through the time we spend with the person who loves us best. We need to be very careful in choosing with whom we're going to spend the most time. God opens up all the time in the world to us, to be with us, to enjoy us and for us to enjoy him. He has given himself over to us, so that we can discover the benefits of the fullness of relating with him. We don't have to worry about the fervency of our devotion. It's not the temperature. It's the time we spend together that changes us.

Before we accept the love of God that comes through Jesus, we are in conflict. We can recognize and know the right thing to do, but we can find ourselves passing by, not so much doing wrong as neglecting to do what's right. The Spirit will begin to open us up to God and others, by repairing the broken communication lines. The Spirit will begin to speak within us, plainly, clearly and as it does that, we are shifted into being new creatures. The Spirit shapes us to become like Jesus, Christlike because we learn to want to be like him and start making choices that reflect the time we've spend in his presence.

We're told in Gal 5:22–23:

> But the fruit of the Spirit is love, joy, peace, forbearance, kindness, goodness, faithfulness, gentleness and self-control. Against such things there is no law.

The Spirit of God takes up residence within us like a plant that we do not have to tend or nurture. Our responsibility is to cooperate with and not to inhibit its growth. The longer the Spirit is within us, the greater the communication between our souls and God. God begins to speak into our souls, to show them how he responds to the troubles in the world and in other people's lives. As he does that, like being in a loving relationship, we begin to act in harmony with the one who loves us. More than that we begin to move in response and to act in partnership with God and God's ways in others' lives. The image that is used in our Scripture above is that the Spirit's attitude and nature grows within us like fruit. We don't have to cultivate this tree. We just need to avoid working against it. The simplest way to do that is by loving and spending time with God.

As we can do that, we see the fruit of the Spirit develop in the relationships we have with God and with other people. All of these aspects of the character of Jesus grow within us. We begin to love others as we love ourselves. We rejoice in all we are seeing, as if for the first time. We relax into an assurance that is deeply peaceful. We give others room to grow and to hear God's voice in their own lives. We treat others as if we and they are of one kind, displaying kindness that shows we're all the same. The way we act in others' lives brings them good and feels good. We become trustworthy to those who count on us. We approach all circumstances with a lighter touch, so we can better understand before we act. We move with a sense of personal control of ourselves that is built on integrity rather than power.

We change.

We aren't responsible to cultivate or work to develop these things; we just make sure we don't work against them. It is crucial to not get in the Spirit's work of developing us. For a while I felt like I was growing as I should, but then came a season where I decided I could handle an issue on my own. There was a time when a man in a church where I worked was telling me over and over how lousy I was. I was a poor pastor, poor leader, had no real concept of how to lead a church. He made it clear that he was going to work to get me out of the church. He repeated this to me in all sorts of ways, both publicly and privately. Things did start to fall apart in that church, regardless of the strides we were making to become sound and healthy. I learned that others were working to undermine my authority and to call my abilities into question. I felt like there was no one in whom I could trust, finally. When two other people told me that they were going to work to see me end my ministry there, I gave up. I decided to resign.

At my last meeting with the Elders of that congregation, I strategized my vengeance on the one man whom I believed had become a force behind much of what I was experiencing. I made one of the worst decisions of my life in trying to see him removed from being an elder as I was leaving the church. Fortunately, the rest of the elders recognized what I was doing and called me on it, rejecting my attempt. It was a demeaning and heart-breaking moment for me because I acted in such an un-Christlike manner to someone I should have loved. In preparation for that last meeting, I had given up bringing my decision to God. I gave up seeking wisdom. I just made my plans without spending any time with God. I didn't spend almost any time with the soap. I paid a price for that both internally in my spirit and among my friends. I came back to the man, some few weeks later, confessed and asked for his forgiveness, which, very graciously, he gave me.

The experience sent me back to God, humbled. I simply spent months asking, "What do you want me to learn in this time," and then paying attention. It was a healing time. It was a time of recognizing I needed to be in a place where the Spirit could move in me. It was a time where I just learned to get out of the way.

Throughout the centuries Christians have discovered and used a number of simple practices that assist us in avoiding getting in God's way. These practices don't develop the fruit of the Spirit. They keep us from slowing them down. They are commonly called *spiritual disciplines*.

One list of these comes from Richard Foster. We can find it in the table of contents of his book—*Celebration of Discipline*. Although I appreciate his descriptions of these practices, I haven't used them here.

Meditation –	spending time with a particular Scripture or aspect of God's world and allowing ourselves to learn everything we can from it by exploring it from within ourselves
Prayer -	talking with God regularly, consistently, throughout our days
Fasting -	removing food from our focus and using mealtimes to focus on the person of God and God's call in our lives on how to live or what to learn
Study -	Reading and re-reading Scripture, digging into its meaning, purpose and design; and paying attention to the world, nature, other people, the life of relationships
Simplicity -	giving up the variety of things the world offers and discovering what is necessary for living
Solitude -	getting away from everything and everyone for periods of time so that we can more easily learn to hear our souls and hear God's Spirit within our souls
Submission -	learning from others and following the guidance of the Holy Spirit as we do that
Service -	giving of ourselves to others, using what we have to benefit them, even when we need it ourselves
Confession -	admitting to God what God already knows; admitting to others what they need to know about us, especially when we err in our relationship with them
Worship -	joining with a community of believers in rejoicing in God's goodness and joy; doing that on our own as well
Guidance -	seeking out the learning of those who are further along the path of spiritual growth and integrity; allowing our hearts to be taught by the Spirit through other people
Celebration -	rejoicing always with God and with others; building opportunities for celebration with those with whom we share the faith

All of these are the ways we spend time with the soap. I want to emphasize that these practices are not what makes us pure. They just help us get ourselves out of the way. As we practice them, they open our souls to

God's Spirit, which, in turn allows our faith, our relationship or connection with God to grow deeper, stronger. It's important to make sure that we understand that this isn't the way some people normally use the word "faith," as something we believe in or trust perhaps even without proof. Faith is not some amount of belief that we might "buck up." Faith is a relationship. When we have a relationship with someone, we have faith in them. We trust that they will act or be as we expect them to be, and we live according to that expectation. That kind of relationship is also what changes us. Spiritual disciplines or practices help us get ourselves, our opinions, and attitudes out of the mix in our relationship with God. They create a gentle "disinterest" in ourselves and help us to listen more carefully to the Spirit and to get out of the way of what the Spirit wants to do within us. The flowing water of the Spirit of God mixed with the presence of God as the soap makes us ready to go into the places where the people God loves dearly are trying to survive. The disciplines are like scrubbing with our hands to make sure we reach every part of ourselves.

We must be careful not to focus on spiritual disciplines as the means to make us more Christlike, that if we just do them more and more that they will make us pure. They can become an idol as easily as anything else. We can start using them to gain control over our mind or body, and pretty soon the practice demands that we submit to it, rather than being a means of spending time with the one who loves us best. We want better communication rather than proof that we're being good or religious. I believe a more useful approach to spiritual disciplines is in seeing them help us in our reactions and responsiveness.

Let me explain how I view these differently from some others. Suppose we build a calendar of spiritual disciplines in which we regulate ourselves. We have certain times of the week or year when we fast or go off into solitude. We have particular times each day when we pray or study or meditate. We set up a regular schedule of service to others, helping out at a food pantry on Tuesdays and Saturdays, let's say. We go to worship once or twice a week. We join the committees that help plan large events—concerts, dinners, etc.—at the church. You get the idea.

These are great habits in which we can enjoy God's presence and mix with the community of the faithful. But the disciplines are to make us more responsive to God's Spirit, especially when the Spirit calls us to respond to participate, to partner with God in an immediate moment. The disciplines should make our response to God's guidance a habit. The purpose of the discipline isn't to keep practicing them. We aren't told that Jesus had a regular forty days each year when he went off to fast and pray. He was led by the Spirit to do that once. Jesus didn't just pray at particular times either, it seems. Jesus prayed, probably all the time.

There was a moment where Jesus has taken three of his disciples, Peter, James and John off and when they return to the rest of the twelve disciples, they find them arguing with teachers of the Law. This story is found in Mark 9:14–29.

The story goes that when Jesus asks what the argument is over, a man steps forward and shares that his son is possessed by an evil spirit. The man explains the symptoms the boy exhibits, and they sound very much like epilepsy. Without going into the details of the story, Jesus removes the spirit from the boy, heals him, and returns him to his father well. Later, the disciples ask why they couldn't heal the boy and Jesus says, "This kind can only come out through prayer."

The difficulty with that moment is that Jesus isn't seen praying. He doesn't stop to pray. He doesn't step away for a moment. He doesn't call out to God. That makes it plain that Jesus' prayer was simply said within himself. He talked with God without it being known to anyone else. Jesus did have a habit of stepping off to talk with God, but Jesus also just talked with God, at any time. This echoes Paul's words from 1 Thess which my atheist friends found so demanding: "pray continually."

We are to pray the best we can, but the good news is that beyond our prayers, the Spirit prays for us—Rom 8:26:

> In the same way, the Spirit helps us in our weakness. We do not know what we ought to pray for, but the Spirit himself intercedes for us through wordless groans.

The Spirit is always talking with God on our behalf so that we can be filled with hope and the knowledge of the presence of God, and the Spirit can grow up within us, recreating us so its fruit becomes evident in our lives. It will call us into prayer, so we don't need to rely only on a particular time for prayer. That's a great practice, but it should also be conversational. It should just be going on all the time and at any time. The more we pay attention to the presence of God, the more we'll recognize when God is speaking to us through his Spirit.

Jesus calls his disciples "little faiths" at times. We translate that as something like, "O ye of little faith," but he uses this as a descriptive of those who began following him. It might describe us as well. People who are "little faiths" don't have much of a regular relationship, a conversational relationship, with God. We are called to be people of faith, people who know and trust God because we talk with God always, because we know that God is constantly present. At the same time, we also need to be people of faith who know when to shut up and listen. When we want to get God right, we need to listen. It is supposed to be a conversation.

This brings us back to Moses telling the people to *hear* in Deut 6:4–6:

> Hear, O Israel: The Lord our God, the Lord is one. Love the Lord your God with all your heart and with all your soul and with all your strength. These *instructions* that I give you today are to be on your hearts.

Hearing the Spirit is the most important aspect of growing into Christlikeness. Focusing our hearts and minds through meditation, study, prayer and fasting can help us to get the distractions of the world and within ourselves to quiet. These are important and useful practices through which we can grow into paying attention daily, at any moment. We can pay attention to what comes to mind and talk with God about it. As we do that, we can begin to recognize the Spirit's voice. It may not be just a random and curious thought that just popped into our head. It may be a word from the Spirit, that God is bringing to mind so that we deal with it in our hearts or lives. If you ever have a question over whether this is God speaking to you or just your conscience, just ask. "Is that you, God? If so . . . then do it again . . . say it to me again, even in another way, so I recognize that it is you." Then go on with your day, allowing yourself to be open to God speaking his direction again.

We can recognize when God is speaking into our day and calling us into action. God can then call us to step away from the world into solitude. God can guide us into focusing our attention on some particular aspect of faith or life in the world, and call us to fast and to focus so that we can understand it or engage with it more deliberately or more specifically as God needs. The Spirit can tell us that it is now time to study.

Some people can't live this way. They need the calendar to keep them steady. I'm not speaking against that. I'm just saying that we must be wary of our practices becoming a commander rather than a guide. When the practice becomes an assurance of piety or purity, we have lost the direction of the practice. The earliest desert fathers and mothers were people who went off into solitude to be in the presence of God. One of the earliest, Anthony, moved out into the desert but was found by those who wanted to learn from him. The story goes that he moved farther away. His purpose was purity and solidarity with God, but he cut himself off from relationships, from community. Although we can learn much from Anthony and the others who went off into the desert, we must recognize that some of them did not grow in relationship with others. It is within relationships with other people that God's most profound work is found. We must find the balance between being with God in spiritual practices and the change of the disciplines to shape us into Christlikeness versus doing the practice for the sake of being "good" for God.

If it is easier for someone to log in a schedule for prayer time than do it. For others who recognize that talking with God continually opens their hearts and that it is easy, do that. The point of any spiritual practice is to become disinterested in our own agenda and to learn what's on God's mind. When we begin to hear God's voice, we then become partners in ministry and in healing the world, and that's the point. We want to learn to hear God. Once we begin hearing God, the soap and water, we can be shaped into Christlikeness.

Chapter Thirteen

Be Mature As Your Father Is Mature

THE POINT OF HEARING God, learning to hear God, is to mature in our relationship with God. It is to grow into Christlikeness so that we partner with God in bringing healing to our world. This is different than being "good." It's different than just rote or severe obedience. It's different from seeking emotionally gripping experiences of worship. We don't get mature by hanging out at church or with Christians. We gain maturity by living our relationship with God, our faith, in the world, and especially with people who don't know or believe in God.

Maturity is being transformed by the work of the Holy Spirit into someone who is actually following and living like Jesus with those who are put off by, angry at, or confused about God, or even those who are consumed in trying to be good enough for God. As we read in Matt 16:24–26:

> Then Jesus told his disciples, "If anyone would come after me, let him deny himself and take up his cross and follow me. For whoever would save his life will lose it, but whoever loses his life for my sake will find it. For what will it profit a man if he gains the whole world and forfeits his soul? Or what shall a man give in return for his soul?

Giving up our lives may include dying, but for most Christ followers it will mean not living for ourselves. It's not fitting Christ into our lives or adding Christ onto what we do. It's living for others through becoming Christlike. The maturity required of such a life is built through a conversational relationship with God. It's built through the constancy of relating to a God who is continually present, continually engaged in seeing how we can partner with him in the lives around us and supplying us with the power to accomplish anything he calls on us to do.

Maturity, for most people, comes through healing. I mean that most of us grow up without a thought toward maturing, and so we make mistakes. We break stuff, we get burned emotionally or, even, physically, and we burn others. We disappoint, cheat, get neglected or are damaged in multiple ways. For most people, this isn't at the level of destroying our psyches, but it is at the level of deep pain. From this pain we make alternative choices, we take more time, we learn what works, and we apply that knowledge. For some this leads into healthy and sustainable lives that reflect a more mature understanding of life and the world.

Spiritual maturity is another thing entirely. It develops through partnership with God. It's something I wish to attain but cannot claim. I continue to grow and to need to grow. My conversation with the young woman on the plane displays that. My failure in trying to hurt the elder displays that. There are times when I know I'm being prompted to move on behalf of God and I'll argue, stop, or even ignore it. There are too many times in my life when I come back to God asking for another opportunity, a chance to follow through as I know I should have. The thing that keeps me hopeful is that I receive the prompts, I learn, and I do better at times.

I have been betrayed many times in my life. That created a wariness, even a fear, in moving into relationships or in following the Spirit into places. I trusted that God knew me, and what he was working within me. That assurance and not seeking a level of purity instead of knowledge of God may have been the soil that produced a change over a number of years. I recognize a greater ease and comfort in following, joyfully obeying, and partnering with God. I am no longer afraid to be disliked. The closer I get to God, the more I recognize that I am different, without making efforts to make myself different.

So, what is Christian maturity?

It's a personal development that reflects and resembles the relationship Jesus had with God and the character of Jesus expressed toward other people. This is a gift of the Holy Spirit to us that grows in us primarily through time spent with God and in a community of believers. Paul spells this out in Eph 4 where he writes,

> . . . I urge you to live a life worthy of the calling you have received. Be completely humble and gentle; be patient, bearing with one another in love. Make every effort to keep the unity of the

Spirit through the bond of peace. There is one body and one Spirit, just as you were called to one hope when you were called; one Lord, one faith, one baptism; one God and Father of all, who is over all and through all and in all.

. . . So Christ himself gave the apostles, the prophets, the evangelists, the pastors and teachers, to equip his people for works of service, so that the body of Christ may be built up until we all reach unity in the faith and in the knowledge of the Son of God and become mature, attaining to the whole measure of the fullness of Christ.

Then we will no longer be infants, tossed back and forth by the waves, and blown here and there by every wind of teaching and by the cunning and craftiness of people in their deceitful scheming. Instead, speaking the truth in love, we will grow to become in every respect the mature body of him who is the head, that is, Christ. From him the whole body, joined and held together by every supporting ligament, grows and builds itself up in love, as each part does its work.

If we have given up living under commandments, and instead have given ourselves over to learning from God how to live, guided by his instructions, we walk in humility. We give ourselves over to seeking God's wisdom and God's voice, which leads us into taking time with understanding and supporting each other. Our spirits calm. The voice of the one who loves each of us speaks into us in a regular conversational manner. As a community then, we are given leaders whose responsibilities focus first on helping each of us learn the tools, perspectives, and strength to serve one another. In this safer environment, we get to practice this deepening care and partnership with God and each other. Our service, joint and general, then strengthens every member of the community, what Paul refers to as the "body" or "the body of Christ." This strengthening joins us into a whole that grows into maturity. As a community, we display a new experience of people living in the world, as we were created to live. We become a new society.

Not sure how you experience that description, but it feels pretty much like a dream to me. In a world where churches are rocked by the scandals of leadership, where Christians tie their hopes and dreams onto politicians of any stripe, where communities split and split again over doctrine—to say nothing of the general atmosphere that's developed with polarization, demonizing, dismissal, bigotry, and plain hatred—isn't the idea of Christian maturity and living in a community of mature Christians a dream?

I think it depends on what we're trying to build. We've told ourselves that the point of church is a building, where people come, rather than a community that's let loose in the world. Jesus didn't send us out into the world to build buildings. We've worked hard at building organization, order, and structure. We haven't worked as hard at building friendship. In Matt 28:19–20, Jesus said,

> Therefore go and make disciples of all nations, baptizing them in the name of the Father and of the Son and of the Holy Spirit, and teaching them to obey everything I have commanded you. And surely I am with you always, to the very end of the age."

One legitimate and alternative way to translate these words is "go and make disciples of all nations, immersing them in the teaching of the Father, the Son and the Holy Spirit, and in everything I have instructed you." The choice of developing friendship should be easily discovered and foundationally involved in our acts of service. We're not just doing nice things to be nice or because we're "commanded" to love our neighbor. We've been instructed that loving and being in relationship with our neighbors is the nature of the world God created. Our acts of service should include learning who the people are whom we serve. We should be learning their stories, understanding their circumstances, spending time with them. Our leaders, apostles, evangelists, prophets, pastors, and teachers should be speaking the natural process of friendship into their guidance, because the people who are served should be seen justly, rightly, as having deep value.

The reason for all this is that this is the highest level of relationship Jesus brings into the life of the earliest disciples. At the Last Supper, Jesus said to them, "I no longer call you servants . . . instead I call you friends" (John 15:15). If this is where the work, person, and teaching of Jesus leads to, we need to be the ones who follow it most closely. Friendship is the core direction of Christian maturity. We are to learn to become friends with the rest of the population.

When we hear about those who are recognized as foundational leaders of faith, Abraham and Moses, we're told that Abraham was a friend of God (Isa 41:8) and that God spoke with Moses "face to face, as a man does with his friend" (Exod 33:11). Friendship has always been the nature of a relationship with God. Because Jesus calls his disciples into this level of friendship as he comes to the end of their time together, when he has shared everything he "heard from [the] Father," we realize they are reaching a level of maturity. This maturity only grows deeper and into fullness when they go through the trauma of Christ's death, the overwhelming impact of his resurrection, and then the indwelling of the Holy Spirit (Acts 2).

It's after the Spirit comes upon them and takes up residence within them that they begin to move away from the self-centered expectation that God's work is only with the Jews. They reach out into the world, which is the story of Acts. What is happening as the Gospels end, Acts happens, and the rest of the New Testament displays is that God's intention to express his heart fully comes about. God always intended to do this with friends, partners who loved him. That's the promise he made to Abraham, that he would bless the world through their relationship (Gen 12:3).

Over and over, we find God speaking into the lives of people, throughout the Bible, calling them into relationship that should affect those around them with insight into the nature of God. God calls them to be a blessing and to produce a blessing. God provides them with wisdom and instruction. God challenges them to be different from the rest of the world and to display that this difference comes through the relationship they have with him. God calls them back to him as they wander, retells them of his love, and promises forgiveness and welcome even if they leave.

We turned all of this into exclusivity and division, rather than engagement, partnership, and life. We chose being "right" over loving. We chose breaking down the truth of God into verses and forcing people to understand and accept them in the same manner we do. Instead of allowing God to speak into our hearts as God can, we have turned to the book and placed our own tone of voice onto the words we find there. We have such difficulty hearing the tone of voice Jesus was that we take his words as fostering new commandments and regulations. We can't seem even to hear his new "instruction" to love as we have been loved.

Christians have almost no voice to bring into the world. For the most part, we are powerless. Some have money and some have position or authority, but these don't hold much weight when we live in a world that promotes "shouting" as the means to demonstrate truth. The world calls us to choose to be significant, while Christ calls us to love others into significance. Our voice is chiefly felt in personal conversation, care, and in presence. When we try to shout our way into making the world the way we think it should be "under God," we just become another group of loudmouths. We demonstrate that we are just as afraid to not be seen as everyone else in the world. Instead of working in quiet, working without others noticing, learning the worth of others and teaching them to understand their worth, we try to make ourselves comfortable with the laws of the country. The most important work we can do begins one-on-one, with those who don't think anyone sees them.

Chapter Fourteen

Becoming Friends

In Tampa, Florida, I was watching the news one evening when a man who runs a number of strip clubs in the city was interviewed. Essentially, he began announcing that, during the week of the Super Bowl, his clubs would be open twenty-four hours a day. This was broadcast as if it is a newsworthy item that the greater community should know. Watching it felt like I was watching a commercial.

How do Christians respond to a situation like this? One way might be to protest. Believers might gather with signs outside the clubs, picket, embarrass people trying to get in, make it difficult for business to happen. It might be a hassle for the owners of the clubs for a while, but, after a little while, protesters will need to get on with their lives and the clubs will flourish again. Another way to respond might be to go to the city council, demanding laws be changed to shutter these businesses, maybe even getting on the council to seek to change the law from the inside.

A small group of Christians took another approach. Several years ago, a group of young adults went off to the Philippines to help in a ministry that guided sex-workers off the streets and into healthy lives. At some point they realized they could be doing this at home, back in Tampa, so they came back. They began a small ministry that was built on the ideas they learned in Asia. They went out on the streets at night, met and made friends with women who were prostituting themselves, gained their trust, and then gave them a home base from which to grow a new life.

In a house their church bought, they gathered a group of these women together and taught them to care for each other through their care of them.

Churches in the area supported this ministry with funds as well as with meals and clothes and even lessons. Eventually, the ministry, called "Created," grew to more houses. They took over a small motel whose rooms became "apartments" for women graduating out of the program. They helped women gain life skills and empowerment by, essentially, becoming friends who worked to establish new life through community.

Like many cities, Tampa also had a large population of homeless or transitory people. A man coming out of that population, as well as out of addiction, came to faith and then turned around to go back to the ones he left. He knew them and the way their lives worked. One of the things that impacted him was the number of programs, support, and resources that were available for women but weren't as readily available to men. With the help of his church and others, he began a ministry to help homeless men discover a new life. He started a construction firm out of the house where he helped guys work into consistently healthy living and choices. It's called "The Timothy Initiative" and it helps guys break free of addictions, grow through honest labor, and discover the tools to contribute to others, securing their own hearts and souls as well as to benefit their families.

I could point to other places in the world, ministries that are focused first on friendship and trust, and then on building life and skills, all the while incorporating the love of God, but these two seem to say a good deal. Their primary focus is in building relationships and community. The best of churches act the same way. They aren't places that are built to be institutions; they're built to form connections between people and people and then between people and God.

And the foundational aspect of this is kindness. Kindness is when we act as if we are the same *kind* as the people we are helping. We are acting in a way we hope someone would act with us if we were in this situation. When we read that God approaches with, knows we need, and extends over generations *loving kindness*, we're reminding ourselves that we were made in the image of God. We are of a kind, us and God, at least from God's point of view. So, as we are with others on our planet, we are reminded to look at them as being of the same kind as us.

Too many times people launch into "helping" by deciding what someone needs, rather than getting to know them and allowing them to tell us what they need. I know a pastor who worked in Kensington, a rough neighborhood in Philadelphia. He told me of church groups that would come with their ideas of how they could help him in his ministry there. They brought puppet shows and street theater. They came and announced they would paint the basement of his church so he could hold classes there. They came with all their best suggestions, and they left filled with assurance that they had done a great job. This wasn't kindness.

He got used to outside groups coming with what they had and what they *knew* would be a benefit to him, but no one stopped to get to know him, to get to know the area, or the neighbors of the church. When the ministry I was working with then came to offer to run a kids' program and a youth program and to teach his people how to lead a youth program, he said, "Sure! That's great! Do whatever you want." We kept asking him if there was anything we should know, or if he wanted us to do it some certain way, and he kept saying, "Whatever you do will be fine." At the end of the first summer we worked with him, we asked for an evaluation. We had noticed there were a ton of kids in the neighborhood, but only a few came to our kids' programs. He said, "Well, that's because kids in this neighborhood are up until 11 or so at night because it's so noisy in the city. People are all outside because it's cooler in the evenings. The kids are sleeping in the morning in the summer." We asked why he didn't tell us that. We could have run the program in the afternoons. That was when he told us of the other groups that had come to "help" his church. He said he had gotten so used to people just coming and doing stuff he didn't think we'd pay attention to him. After that he told us every way he thought we could help best. The next summer we did our kids' programs in the afternoon, and we had more kids than we could handle almost. The pastor had gotten used to not being treated with kindness, so he reflected that as we tried to show him we were ready to listen. Once he found out our sincerity, he was ready to guide us into providing our best efforts.

Kindness is the foundation of friendship. It is knowing and acting on the understanding that we are of a kind. Jesus, as the tone of voice of God, took the time to demonstrate that he knows what we are going through here. He knows we need company when we are in trauma, or struggling, or just bugged with life. One of the first things we learn about Jesus is that he was known as *Emmanuel*, that is, "God with us." The first step of healing and kindness is "I'm here with you." Jesus' whole life and teaching and death is telling us that truth . . . *I am here with you.* His resurrection is the proof of his being the voice of God, and the way we should hear God.

Friendship is the basis of joy, and that is the direction in which God is leading us. God wants us to discover the joy in his heart, so that we can know it fully in ours. In John 15: 10–11, Jesus told his friends,

> If you keep my *instructions*, you will remain in my love, just as I have kept my Father's *instructions* and remain in his love. I have told you this so that my joy may be in you and that your joy may be complete.

That word "complete" carries a sense of "being filled," like over and over. The joy we are to experience is one that should be renewed regularly. That kind of joy is found when we act as if we are of a kind and that kindness is experienced as friendship.

Imagine that you enter a room where there are some three hundred people all talking with each other. It could be a seminar, a gala dinner, some gathering to hear a speaker, but everywhere you look there are people in pairs up to small groups of six or eight who are focused on each other, talking and listening. As you scan the room, you don't see any place to connect or fit in, and this little voice in your head begins telling you that you should cut out. "This isn't a place for you. Why did you come?"

Just then a hand shoots up on the other side of the room and even before your eyes are focusing on the hand, you're already feeling different. You look in the direction, and then you experience a smile, and then you see the eyes above the smile, and you realize that it is one of your best friends. They're waving you over and then they are standing as you make your way through the crowd. Inside you're already feeling that you're glad you came, that you're wanted, and that you are supposed to be here. Even before you're beside them getting a hug. That experience is joy. It's when we see someone's face light up with the knowledge of our presence. This is the experience of coming to Jesus.

People call it "being born again." We are in trouble, we feel alone, we are insecure and even have a sense of dread and then someone wants us. The young man I wrote about earlier, who came to the Sunday school class and didn't enter but made sure that we connected. It was first eye to eye, but then it was face to face. He came hoping he would be wanted and discovered he was, and he didn't have to fit into the schedule of the class. He was important in and of himself. Life was better, even amid his turmoil. He, later, discovered that greater and more far-reaching experience of Jesus wanting him, and he felt that life became brand-new, suddenly.

The message of Jesus' being with us is that God knows us, hurts as we are separated from him, seeks out every avenue to demonstrate grace and love to us, and provides us with the means of being healed and made whole again. For most people who accept this expression of love, it does feel like being born again, like we're able to see things that were always there, but we simply didn't experience them or experience them in all their fullness. There are a host of ways that God's face "lights up" when we experience God's presence, but all of them express the depth of his desire to be in relationship with us.

Ministry that actively expresses the same thing through true kindness, through building friendship, and that moves in the direction of joy mirrors the heart of God. It expresses the tone of voice that is Jesus.

Epilogue

Reality

After a Bible study one day, a man stopped to discuss some of what I said. He told me that he was a bit disturbed by the idea I presented about interpreting the Bible's words. He said, "I never interpret the Bible. I take it just as it is written." I pointed out that the Bible we have is an interpretation as it is a translation from Hebrew and Greek to English. That didn't bother him. It was, as he understood it, the English version and, in fact, the King James Version, that was the "inspired" word of God. He took its expression of the words as the only way to hear God truly.

He didn't come off that opinion even when I pointed out the changes in our language since the time of that early translation, how some of the words we use now mean the opposite of how the translators understood those words then. Didn't bother him. It was still the plain word of God. When I asked about the poetry in the psalms that used phrases like "trees clapping," didn't he have to interpret that. "It's poetry," he said. "Yes," I agreed, "but aren't we interpreting those words and not really thinking that trees applaud." "No," he replied, "we know it's poetry."

There was no changing his mind, but I'm hoping that some of the minds that read this book are changed. I'm hoping that my questions and suggestions have stimulated thinking and praying and even more exploring. I wrote this book with an attitude of conversation, seeking to just get people to consider that there may be a difference in the way to hear the words we've come to know so well. Even the King James Version, as I pointed out earlier, is not saying things the way we have been taught to hear them . . . even with the words that were used there. The translators were saying, and intended to say, that God spoke to the people in the tone of voice of a friend or just a person on the street at the time they translated. If we don't clarify that impression and take hold of the friendliness of God, we're left with a God who hates us if we don't follow his rules exactly.

Jesus came to talk with us so we could hear the tone of voice of God as he expressed how humans should live. He came to demonstrate it as well. He came to show us how to enter the kingdom of God, which opens to us as we know that we have nothing to offer God, not even good advice. We all know what God should do to make life better, or to just make our lives better. We enter the kingdom of God when we realize that we don't even have good advice. All we have is ourselves, as we are. Jesus came to show us that we're wanted by God, just that way . . . angry, fed up, disappointed, crushed, used, bewildered, exhausted, ready and even pretty much okay . . . as far as we can tell.

Jesus came to show us that God is not like some bigger, oversized human being. He taught us that we don't have a God that is going to crush us for making wrong choices, for hurting ourselves or even for hurting others. Through Jesus we now see and believe, instead, that God's heart is crushed, broken, when we choose anything that separates us from God, and this is because God knows the consequences of damaging choices. Through Jesus and the Spirit, God then leads us, instructs us to follow him in knowing and respecting others as we have experienced his knowledge and love of us. And because we recognize that God loves us, regardless of our choices, we can realize that we can love each other . . . even when we seem to be enemies.

Becoming the people who can develop that kind of wisdom and strength, requires us to get to know the one who gave us the instructions, even more than knowing the instructions. Spending time with God, like spending time with the soap, changes us. It changes us so that we can be useful, deeply useful in others' lives.

And that's the point . . . becoming useful in the lives of other people.

There are people who will consider this understanding I've shared and will lift up questions about atrocities in the Bible, some that were attributed to God, or seemingly commanded by God. They will lift up the prospect of hell and the "burning lake of fire," where "the cowardly, the unbelieving, the vile, the murderers, the sexually immoral, those who practice magic arts, the idolaters and all liars" will be sent (Rev 21:8). They will hold these up to ask, but what about *this* God?

Suppose Jesus is God's tone of voice. Suppose we are to listen to God the way Jesus listened to God and spoke about God. What if those who go into the lake of fire or the "second death" as it is also called in Rev 21 actually are dead and gone. They are not held there for all eternity, but simply finish life . . . as the atheists tell us they expect to go. The list above is a list of people who never wanted God and who used other people or other forces to gain power and control. The ideas we look at today of sorcery and magic are not the same as what Paul and the people of his time experienced. In that time, they were deadly and weren't seeking to appreciate the earth or the nature of the universe.

Jesus made plain that we choose hell, not him, not God. We judge ourselves.

For people who "hold out a hope" for hell, that there will be ongoing punishment for those who do wrong, Paul made a similar clarification about judgment in Romans. He lists all, or seemingly all, the ways that people desecrate the ways God would have us live, many of the ways we see people living today, and then concludes, "You, therefore, have no excuse, you who pass judgment on someone else, for at whatever point you judge another, you are condemning yourself, because you who pass judgment do the same things" (Rom 2:1). As we read those words, we may be saying to ourselves that *we* aren't doing those things, but the truth is that we are. Simply because we are acting as someone who is in a position where we can judge.

Can we not judge?!

Of course, we can't. We're in no position to judge. No matter how much we would like to judge, we can't move into that position because it is simply an idol. It is seeking control. It's demanding that life work the way I want it to work, so that I can understand it, so that I can feel safe, so that it will only move in the manner I want it to move . . . so that I'm comfortable and remain comfortable.

We can, instead, recognize what is wrong, live in the other direction, get to know God, and open our hearts, homes, and lives to those who try everything other than God, including all the avenues of control. We can move into their circumstance, alongside them, so that we can hear directly from them how they need help, and then provide the help we can. The only way we will make a serious difference in others' lives is as friends. The only weapons we have in our arsenal are kindness and love.

We are called into a spiritual battle, one in which we are to put on the full armor of God.

In Eph 6 we are told:

> Finally, be strong in the Lord and in his mighty power. Put on the full armor of God, so that you can take your stand against the devil's schemes. For our struggle is not against flesh and blood, but against the rulers, against the authorities, against the powers of this dark world and against the spiritual forces of evil in the heavenly realms.

We're not here to fight against other people but against the evil that wants to divide us from God. As much as we would like to claim that those *other people* are the ones who are evil, we're not given the option of deciding. We're sent in to provide people, everyone, with the experience of an alternative life, an alternative society, a different way of living that's built within the instructions God gave us on how he created human beings to live with each other and with him. It appears that the best and highest way to follow God in Jesus, then, is to become friends.

God didn't call us to live significant lives . . . he calls us to love others into their significance.

Bibliography

Augustine. *Confessions of Saint Augustine*. https://www.acatholic.org/wp-content/uploads/2014/05/confessions-of-Saint-Augustine.pdf.

Foster, Richard. *Celebration of Discipline*. New York: Harper & Row, 1978.

Josephus. *Josephus: The Complete Works*. Translated by William Whiston. Nashville: Thomas Nelson, 1998.

Lewis, C. S. *Mere Christianity*. HarperCollins e-books.

Pascal, Blaise. *Pensées*. Translated by Gianluca Ruffini. Kindle Edition, 2017.

Rosin, Hannah. "How Hollywood Saved God." *The Atlantic*, Dec 2007. https://www.theatlantic.com/magazine/archive/2007/12/how-hollywood-saved-god/306444.

Made in United States
Orlando, FL
03 December 2023

40071008R00078